D1545692

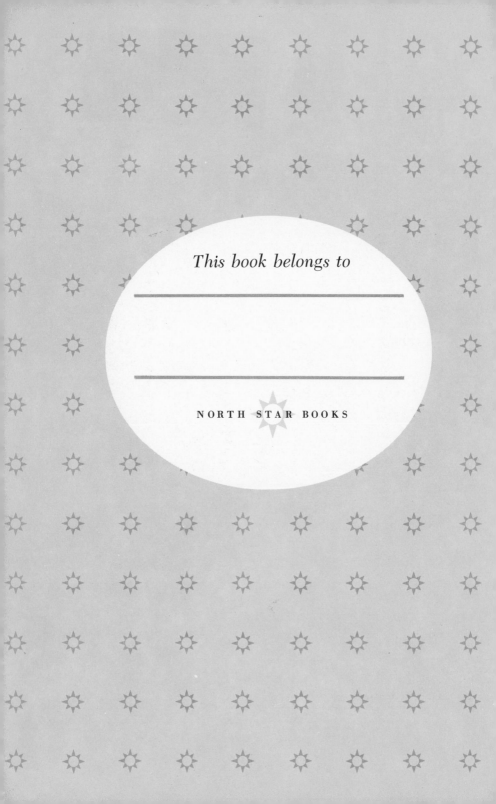

This book belongs to

_____

_____

NORTH STAR BOOKS

976.4
John

Johnson, William Weber

AUTHOR

The Birth of Texas

TITLE

DATE DUE	BORROWER'S NAME	ROOM NUMBER

PROPERTY OF
SAINT MATTHEW SCHOOL

The Birth of
TEXAS

NORTH STAR BOOKS

The Birth of
TEXAS

WILLIAM WEBER JOHNSON

Illustrated by Herb Mott

Houghton Mifflin Company Boston

The Riverside Press Cambridge

Also by

WILLIAM WEBER JOHNSON

Sam Houston, the Tallest Texan

COPYRIGHT © 1960 BY WILLIAM WEBER JOHNSON
ALL RIGHTS RESERVED INCLUDING THE RIGHT TO REPRODUCE
THIS BOOK OR PARTS THEREOF IN ANY FORM.
LIBRARY OF CONGRESS CATALOG CARD NUMBER: 59–9731
THE RIVERSIDE PRESS • CAMBRIDGE
PRINTED IN THE U.S.A.

Contents

Mar. 1966.

No. 21

P.B.
was here

Those who visit Alamo Plaza in modern San Antonio, Texas, are treading on historic ground. On the marble cenotaph are the faces of Davy Crockett, Jim Bowie, Bonham, Travis and other heroes who gave their lives that Texas might be born. The small gray chapel adjoining the plaza is all that is left of the old fort that for thirteen days withstood the memorable siege and bombardment.

Pause for a moment where ivy clings to ancient walls. Perhaps if you listen closely you can faintly hear, above the murmur of the traffic, the rumble of Mexican cannons, the grim reply of tired rifles and the ghostly echo of the Mexican bugler playing the degüello — *the call to attack with no quarter!*

Whenever the odds seem insurmountable, it is well to "Remember the Alamo!"

STERLING NORTH
General Editor

For

Peter

Jane

and

Richard

1

The Napoleon of the West

THE FIRST MONTHS of 1836 were, for the Southwest, cold and disagreeable. Bitter north winds swept down from the High Plains, across the Staked Plains, through the canyons of the Pecos River, down across the cactus-studded desert land that sloped gently to the Rio Grande and then, on the other side, sloped gradually upward to the Sierra Madre Mountains of Mexico.

The north wind brought cold rains, sleet, and sometimes snow. The buffalo and wild Longhorn cattle and mustang horses stood with their rumps to the weather. Wolves and coyotes, winter-thin and weary, moved listlessly and hopelessly, looking hungrily for smaller animals. Wandering bands of Indians stopped their roving, and instead huddled around smoky fires of mesquite wood or buffalo chips. It was a time to stay quiet and wait. In another month or so the grass would become green again. Then there would be game and food and reason to move about.

Some days the wind would drop and the sun would appear, burning the land with a fierce heat. But at night the cold would return — and the Indians and animals knew that winter was not finished, that it was not yet time to stir.

But there were some who could not wait for spring. Advancing slowly northward was a long marching column. The brilliant uniforms of the men and the shining trappings of the horses contrasted with the somber landscape.

First came cavalrymen, mounted on small, spirited Spanish horses. They carried lances with pennants of red, green, and white. Their uniforms were red and blue. Then came a smaller group of men, the officers. Their uniforms were richer. Their swords were sheathed in scabbards chased with silver and gold. Their saddles and harness jingled with silver ornaments. Their boots were high and brightly polished. Most rode their horses. Others rode in fine carriages, lurching across the rough country with their saddle horses tied behind the carriage.

Then came columns of thousands of marching men.

Their uniforms were of cheap gray cotton and were poorly fitted. Many of the men wore blankets, or serapes, around their shoulders. They had stiff black military caps, and some wore marching boots. But more went barefooted, carrying their boots slung across their shoulders, their callused feet more comfortable on the rough, stony land than they would have been in shoes.

Along with the foot soldiers lumbered ox-drawn carts carrying supplies for the army — hay for the horses, corn, beans, and chile peppers for the common soldiers, fine foods and wines for the officers. There were light field cannon, supplies of lead for molding rifle and cannon balls, and sack after leather sack of gunpowder.

Last in the column trudged hundreds of women and children, families of many of the foot soldiers, struggling along under burdens of blankets, cooking braziers, and sacks of charcoal. In the Mexican army each soldier, or *soldado,* could bring along his wife, or *soldadera,* to cook and care for him, and many did.

At night the soldiers and their families cooked around their own small fires and rolled themselves in blankets to sleep on the ground. The animals were turned loose to try to find food in the barren country. Each morning when the eastern sky was faintly gray, officers would ride back along the column, shouting to the soldiers to prepare to march. The soldiers would arise, stiff with cold and unable to speak through chattering teeth.

Day after day they would find that some of the animals, exhausted with fatigue and near starvation, had fallen to the ground during the night. Some would have died; others were too weak to rise again and could only be left behind for the buzzards that each day came in greater numbers to wheel in the sky over the slowly advancing column. The animals that survived had to carry heavier and heavier loads.

Sometimes the women and children — and sometimes the soldiers too, although they were somewhat
better equipped — would fall by the road. They would
beg the officers to send doctors and medicines. But
the army, although it carried cases of wine and trunks
of dress uniforms for the officers, had few medicines
and fewer doctors.

The women tried brewing tea from strange herbs
to cure the aches, fevers, and chills. Many of them
carried their sick children in their arms until they died
and were buried under little mounds of stones at the
side of the trail. Graves could not be dug in the frozen

ground. When the women themselves became too ill to walk, they had to be left — prey for the wolves and coyotes.

The men could not help this. They were soldiers; they had to obey orders. Their officers, in trying to speed them on the difficult march, frequently repeated that their general had promised each of them a decoration — the Legion of Honor. Each at the end of the campaign was to receive a medal inscribed "Honor, Valor, and Country." No one, they were told, could wear the medal unless he had helped suppress the rebellion of the infidel Texans who dared to defy the Republic of Mexico and its leader, its President and Commander-in-Chief — General Antonio Lopez de Santa Anna.

Santa Anna himself rode near the head of the column. His was the handsomest horse, his the finest uniform. When the road was smooth and he was weary of the saddle, he rode, lounging on velvet cushions, in a shining carriage drawn by matched horses. At night he slept in a tent on a silk-covered bed. On a table at his bedside he always kept the same things: a snuff-box with the initial *N* enclosed in a wreath; a short sword with the same initial; some gilt buttons and a morocco-leather writing case. All were mementos of Napoleon, whom Santa Anna greatly admired. He even referred to himself as the "Napoleon of the West," but he was, in his own mind, a greater man than Napoleon. Where Napoleon had failed he would triumph. He, Santa Anna, was not a man to be trifled with. Once he had suppressed the Texas rebellion he might lead his victorious army on to Washington, the capital of the Yankee nation. So he told his officers.

Behind his tent Santa Anna kept crates of fighting chickens. In the evenings when things were dull in camp he would pit one fighting cock against another, inviting his officers to bet with him on the outcome — an outcome that he almost always knew in advance. They were his chickens.

2

Marked for Revenge

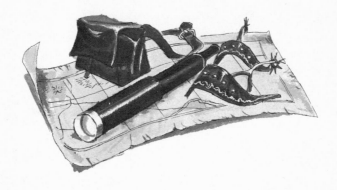

THE OBJECTIVE toward which Santa Anna and his army were driving was a Texas frontier town, San Antonio de Bexar. Originally it had been nothing more than a sleepy mission settlement, founded by priests in 1718 to civilize and convert the Indians.

Now it was a bustling town, full of excitement and a sense of danger. San Antonio was the most important station on the Camino Real, or King's Road, that led from Old Mexico to United States territory in Louisiana. It separated two very different worlds. To the south and west lay Mexico, a country that had only recently won its independence from Spain and still clung to many Old World ways. To the east and north lay the territory of the United States, a young,

vigorous, and land-hungry nation.

The frontier territory was known as Texas, so named for the Tejas Indians that Spanish explorers had found there. The Indian word *tejas* meant "friendly." And to the ambitious settlers from the United States, it was a friendly land indeed. Game was plentiful—buffalo, deer, antelope, wild turkeys. There were wild cattle and horses to be had. There was a wealth of native food—grapes, plums, persimmons, cherries, haws, dewberries, walnuts, pecans, and hickory nuts, and hollow trees filled with honey. There were plains thick with grass for grazing, and the soil, once turned with a plow, was rich and productive.

The government of the newly independent Mexico had for a time been hospitable to emigrants from the United States, giving them land for farming or grazing, allowing them to import goods from the United States duty-free, exempting them from taxes until they became settled. Immigrants swarmed in by the thousands, until the eastern half of what we now know as Texas was more like the United States than Mexico, of which it was still a part. Although many of the settlers sincerely tried to be good citizens of Mexico, it became more and more difficult. For Mexico was moving farther and farther away from democracy. In 1833 Santa Anna was elected President of Mexico and

almost immediately became a dictator. Harsh meas-
ures were imposed and many of the guarantees that
had been offered the Texas settlers were withdrawn.
The Texans became increasingly rebellious, and there
were skirmishes between the settlers and the Mexican
soldiers sent to discipline them.

In the fall of 1835 Santa Anna had sent his brother-
in-law, Martin Perfecto de Cos, to Texas with an army
of 1200 men to punish the Texans for their mutinous
acts. Cos announced that he would overrun Texas
and expel all settlers who had come there since 1830.
A volunteer army of 300 Texans stormed into San
Antonio, forced Cos and his much larger army to
surrender, and released them on a promise that they
would retreat beyond the Rio Grande and stay there.
Some of the adventurous men who made up the little
Texas army remained in San Antonio, knowing well
that the fighting wasn't finished yet, that Santa Anna
would not easily accept such a defeat. Some, more
reckless than the rest, set out for the Mexican town of
Matamoros on the Rio Grande, determined to seize it.
They took with them the best of the equipment. Still
others returned to their farms.

The center of military operations at San Antonio
was the Alamo, a presidio, or fortress, built on the
eastern outskirts of the settlement. Originally it had

been the Mission of San Antonio de Valero — a cluster of buildings of stone and adobe brick. As San Antonio de Bexar became an important outpost, first of Spain and later of Mexico, the priests in the mission were replaced by soldiers. During Mexico's war of independence the mission-fortress was garrisoned by a company of soldiers from Alamo de Parras in Coahuila, Mexico, and the presidio became known as the Alamo. In Spanish *alamo* means cottonwood tree; both the San Antonio River and the ditches supplying the Alamo with water were bordered with cottonwoods.

The town itself, just to the west of the Alamo, was built around two squares, or plazas — Military Plaza and Constitution Plaza. Between them was the Cathedral of San Fernando and the buildings which housed both the priests and the town government. Around the edges of the two plazas were small shops and beyond them the homes of the town's wealthy and important citizens, large buildings of stone and timber built in the Spanish colonial style. Farther out were the more modest one-story houses of adobe with packed earth floors.

As frontier towns went, San Antonio was busy, crowded, and gay. Mule trains came and went; so did lonely adventurous men who were seeking gold or excitement or trade with the Indians. Wooden-wheeled oxcarts moved in and out of the town. In the homes of the wealthy entertaining was done in the European fashion, with fine linen and silver. In the humble homes cooking was done over tiny charcoal fires, and members of the family slept on the floor. At night there often was the music of guitars and violins, the exciting Spanish music blending with the reels and hoedowns of the American frontier.

This was the town toward which Santa Anna and his army were marching. This was the town marked for revenge.

3

The Tennesseeans

WHILE SANTA ANNA and his army moved slowly toward San Antonio from the south, a party of sixteen men rode toward it from the east. The group had formed in Nacogdoches, on the Louisiana border, under the leadership of David Crockett, the great frontiersman who had until recently been a Congressman from Tennessee.

Crockett, famous for his exploits in the woods and for his speeches in Congress, had been defeated in his last political campaign in Tennessee and was off to seek his fortune in the new land he called "The Texies." In Nacogdoches he had been welcomed with a cannon salute and had been entertained in the finest homes. For these occasions he wore a frock coat and displayed gallant manners. But he was more at home in fringed buckskin clothing, carrying his famous rifle, "Old Betsy." He had gathered around him a group of other ambitious, fame-eager men who had heard of Texas and what was happening there.

They were not all from Tennessee, although Crockett proudly described them as "my Tennessee boys," nor were they all frontiersmen. Some wore buckskin clothing as Crockett did and walked with the easy, swinging gait of forest and mountain men. But others wore frock coats and bright-colored breeches. Some wore plain work clothing. One had a badly scarred face, wore an eyepatch and a seaman's jacket, and spoke knowingly of adventures on the high seas. Crockett and his friends called him "The Pirate," which was probably accurate. Another wore lace cuffs and a high-crowned white flat-topped hat and always smoked a cheroot. At times he would place the white hat on the ground and put three thimbles and a dried pea on the flat top. He would cover the pea with one thimble and then move all three thimbles rapidly, inviting his audience to bet with him on which thimble concealed the pea. No one ever beat him, and Crockett and his companions called him "Thimblerig," for the game at which he was so expert.

As Crockett and his men rode along on the trail

from Nacogdoches to San Antonio, their leader made frequent little speeches from horseback, telling of his oratorical triumphs in Congress and his exploits in the woods and on the trail. But more often he spoke of Texas and their venture.

"All us half-horse, half-alligator men are coming to Texas," he would say, "to fight for our rights. Men with the nobility of the horse and the pure mean cussedness of the alligator, once aroused. And, you might say, the nose of the fox. For us gentlemen adventurers can smell a fight brewing a sight further away than a fox can smell a broody hen.

"You'll see, when we get to San Antonio de

Be'ar, where we're bound—another hundred or so such as us. All following the scent of a fight. They've had one fight and they're like to have another, for they say old Santy Anny will be coming back."

Crockett's party had at first followed the Camino Real, which wasn't a road at all, and in places hardly a trail. Through the pine forests the bare earth was exposed where the hoofs of horses had crushed the pine needles, but on the prairies sometimes the trail was lost completely in tangled grass. At streams and rivers, however, trees were blazed to show where a crossing might be made in safety.

The company of men lived well. There were occa-

sional farms and signs, such as: "George Antonio Dwight Keeps Mustangs & People 1¼ leagues off Right-hand path three times." Crops had been good that year and farmers were glad to feed volunteers who were going to fight for Texas' freedom. There would be dried beef or venison, beans, black-eyed peas, bread made from coarse corn meal, dried fruit, honey, and "long sweetening," or sorghum molasses. They were glad to exchange food and lodging — the visitors usually slept on piles of hay in the barn or stable — for a little cash and whatever news the travelers could provide.

When the men camped on the trail they would eat fresh game, which Crockett insisted on killing personally, deer, wild turkeys, or rabbits. Then they would sit around their fire and tell tales and sing songs like

> "Hurray for the Texas Volunteers!
> We are the boys so handy.
> We'll teach the Mexicans to fear
> Our Yankee Doodle Dandy!"

He was thrown into prison and remained there for two years. Finally released, he returned to his colony, admitting that war was unavoidable. He took a leading part in organizing the volunteer forces for their attack on the Mexican forces in San Antonio in December, and then went to the United States to try to get a loan. Without borrowing money the Texans had no hope of raising and maintaining an army.

San Felipe de Austin was a neat little community, rows of well-made log cabins, a store, and two taverns, where travelers might sleep on the floor. The houses were simple. Some were only one room. Others were really two cabins, joined together by a single roof, with an open "dog trot" between the two buildings.

Two by two Crockett and his men and their horses were ferried across the Brazos River. Crockett was one of the first over.

"Where you bound?" asked the boatman.

Crockett smiled. "Like the song says, to hear a noise and see a fight. And they tell me San Antonio de Be'ar is the best place for both. But we figured we'd stop and pay our respects to Governor Henry Smith."

"He'll be glad of a little respect," said the boatman. "Ain't many people giving him much these days."

The boatman told them how to find the Governor's

4

The Troubled Gover[n]

INSTEAD OF REMAINING on the Camino Real[,]
San Antonio, Crockett's company swung to the [s]
to pass through San Felipe de Austin, which wa[s]
Texas colony's principal headquarters. It was a[n]
settlement on the Brazos River, established a [few]
years earlier by Stephen F. Austin, one of the f[irst to]
lead a party of immigrants into Texas.

Austin and most of his people had tried t[o live]
peacefully and obediently under the laws of M[exico]
and had been loyal to their adopted country[, but]
gradually the older settlers lost faith in Mexic[o. The]
newcomers to the colony almost all favored reb[ellion.]
Austin himself, a peace-loving man, made th[e long]
trip to Mexico City to protest Santa Anna's

cabin. Crockett left word for his men to wait for him on the riverbank, and he set off for the Governor's "office."

The Governor's office was a simple one-room cabin with a floor of split logs. Governor Smith, a large, heavy man with a big mustache, was seated on a raw-hide chair before a small table piled with papers. He held a quill pen and smoothed his mustache with it while he scowled at the papers.

Crockett introduced himself. "We're bound for Be'ar to see if we can be of use, Governor, and thought we'd pay our respects as well as find out what's going on."

"Going on?" The Governor seemed to explode. "Everything is going on and everything is going wrong." He paused, and then went on in a calmer voice. "My apologies, Colonel Crockett. Welcome to Texas. We are happy to have you with us in our fight for freedom and decency. I forgot my manners — but then it's a wonder I do not lose my mind entirely. You know General Houston, of course, being a Tennesseean?"

"Of course, Governor. Who does not know of General Houston? One of the bravest men that ever lived, and a statesman with it. You are most fortunate to have him as commander-in-chief of your armies."

"Armies?" The Governor seemed to explode again. "Rabble. Just rabble, and not even armed rabble. Every man is an army unto himself, and every tenth man is commander-in-chief."

Finally Governor Smith became calm enough to explain how the garrison at San Antonio had been divided and weakened by the Matamoros expedition, which was led first by one officer, then another. The venture was being made against the wishes of himself, the Governor, and General Houston.

The Governor's Council, which was supposed to aid and support Smith, favored the expedition. The Governor ordered the council adjourned, and the council in turn impeached him.

He was continuing to serve as governor and the council constantly impeded him at every step, Smith explained. No one knew where the true authority lay and would not until a constitution could be drawn up. For this purpose a convention was to be held at Washington-on-the-Brazos on March 1. Meanwhile, there was no authority, and Santa Anna was preparing an invasion—perhaps had already started.

Houston had gone to Goliad to try to halt the Matamoros expedition and keep the volunteer soldiers in Texas, where they might be of some use defending the colony against the invasion of Santa Anna. But his authority was ignored and Houston finally had returned to San Felipe de Austin. Governor Smith had given him a furlough until the convention could be held.

So now he had gone off for a visit among his friends the Indians, making certain that they would not ally themselves with the Mexicans, and the Texans were without the one commander who might be able to save them.

Crockett asked who was in charge at San Antonio. There had been so many that it was almost impossi-

SAINT MATTHEW SCHOOL
1015 E. Dayton St.
South Bend, Ind.

ble to say, the Governor replied. First Austin was in charge. Then he left on his mission to the United States, putting Burleson in command. Burleson was all right for a siege but he was little inclined to attack. Colonel Ben Milam led in the storming of the city and was killed. Then General Burleson returned to his family and Colonel Francis Johnson was left in charge. Colonel Johnson returned to San Felipe de Austin and got the authority of the Governor's Council to lead the Matamoros expedition, and Colonel Neill was left in charge. So far as the Governor knew, Colonel Neill was still there, but he couldn't guarantee it. Most of the Texans had gone back to their farms to get in their spring crops — and there was no way of keeping them. There was no money to pay them. Those who remained behind were the volunteers who were either sick or wounded when the Matamoros expedition left, and perhaps a few who were obeying orders. Smith was trying to send reinforcements there, but it was difficult to raise volunteers. The people did not realize the danger. The authorities knew that Santa Anna either would march or was already marching against Texas, but the people would refuse to believe it until there actually was a fight. They would just say "It's more Mexican lies," and let it go at that. By the time they woke up it might be too late.

Crockett thanked Governor Smith and said goodbye. He and his men rode on toward the west, and San Antonio. While they rode Crockett tried to explain to his companions what he had learned from Governor Smith. But it was complicated by strange names and unfamiliar situations.

About all he could make out was that they needed a little time to form a government. "Like a fellow trying to build a hen house with one hand and using a rifle on the wolves with the other."

And they rode along at a faster clip, across wide grassy prairies, through forests of pine and live oak, then later through groves of thorny mesquite trees.

And as they moved westward prickly-pear cactus became common and the country was more open.

Late in the afternoon of the third day after leaving San Felipe de Austin, they descended a gradual slope to a brisk-flowing stream. They forded it, and a little later came to a wide grassy plain where nearly a hundred horses and mules were hobbled. A man on horseback rode over to them.

"Goin' to Be'ar?" he shouted.

Crockett said they were.

"Reckon you'll want to leave your mounts here, then," the man said. "Or you can ride them in and one of you can bring them back. It's a right smart walk. Five, six miles."

Why, asked Crockett, should the horses be left here?

"Everything's short in Be'ar," the man replied. "Including forage for the animals. That's the least problem they've got. The animals can be pastured out here where there's grass aplenty, and water, too. It'd be a blessing if the other shortages could be fixed so easy. Like as if you should find riflemen growing on trees and gunpowder on the vines."

"Are things as bad as that?" asked Crockett.

"That bad and worse," said the man. "You wait and find out for yourself. Too few guns and not enough powder. And they say Santy Anny's coming with ten thousand troops. And our troops fightin' and feudin' among themselves. And nobody knowin' for sure who's in charge."

Crockett smiled and motioned to his followers.

"Come on," he said. "Leave us be on our way and see this delightful place. We will send our horses back."

They followed the sun to the west and soon crested a hill and looked down to a shallow valley. Beyond them was an old mission that formed one corner of a large enclosure, surrounded by thick stone and adobe walls. From within the walls plumes of smoke rose from small fires. A little river, glistening in the late afternoon sun, curved around the mission on the west, and beyond the river was a town.

That, said Crockett, was the Mission of San Antonio de Valero, otherwise known as the Alamo, and beyond the small horseshoe bend in the river was the town of San Antonio de Bexar, where they were bound.

They moved ahead and rode through the open gate of the Alamo.

5

A Company of Volunteers

CROCKETT AND HIS MEN sent their horses back to pasturage and spent that night in the Alamo, sleeping on cornshuck mattresses on the floor of the barracks. The next day they walked into the streets of San Antonio, exchanging rough greetings with other volunteers who were there, puzzling over the Spanish language they heard spoken.

Thimblerig had his game set up, the white hat on the ground, the thimbles moving rapidly on the flat crown. A crowd gathered. Since few of them had any money with which to gamble, he let them write out slips of paper for "one shilling," "un peso," or "one dollar." If they could write they signed their names. If not, they made an X. Thimblerig quickly accumulated a large wad of these slips. He stuffed them into the pocket of his frock coat and said, "If old Santy Anny don't kill us all I'll be a rich man someday. If I live to claim it, and you all live to pay."

"You'd be richer through a bounty of some good Texas bottomland — if you live to claim it," said a bystander.

A man came running through the street shouting, "Attention all! Meeting of all volunteers in the Military Plaza! Meeting of all volunteers in the Military Plaza!"

Thimblerig and his audience moved down the street toward the Military Plaza. Here they found fifty or sixty other volunteers and several hundred Mexicans gathered. Everyone was talking at once, and it was impossible to understand what it was about except that the name of Jim Bowie was mentioned frequently. Bowie was one of the most famous of the Americans in San Antonio. An adventurer, treasure hunter, fighter, and speculator, he had long lived in San Antonio, had married the daughter of the Mexican governor, and had recently lost both his wife and his children in an epidemic of cholera.

One man climbed onto a box in the center of the plaza and waved his arms for attention.

"Quiet, you ring-tailed hyenas, quiet!" he shouted.

The noise from the crowd died down and the man continued.

"I got no authority to be your president or chairman or whatever you call it, but I got a good pair of lungs, and I guess I can explain things as good and as loud as the next man."

"Hooray!" the crowd shouted, and waved their hats in the air — coonskin caps, wool stocking caps, high dress hats, and sloppy felt hats.

"Quiet!" the man roared again. When the crowd became silent he continued.

"Chances are most of you don't know this. But Colonel Neill announced today that he was leaving. There's illness in his family and he is taking indefinite leave."

"Hooray for Colonel Neill!" shouted the men. "Hooray for his family!"

Finally the speaker got them quiet again and went on.

"Colonel Neill has announced that his successor is Colonel Travis." There was a grumble in the crowd. "Now we got nothing against Colonel Travis. He's a good soldier, a good fighting man, and he's shown that he's not scared. But just the same we're citizen soldiers and we got a right to elect our own leaders from among ourselves."

There were yells of approval from the crowd.

"Now I'd like to nominate a man that I'd follow to hell and back. He's a man not afraid of Mexicans nor other varmints. He's fought alligators with his bare hands. He's opposed swordsmen when he was armed with naught but a little knife no bigger than my foot." The man raised a huge foot for his listeners to see. The crowd laughed. "He's beat the Indians at their own game and he's probably kilt more Mexicans than any man here.

"I'd like to nominate Colonel Jim Bowie as our leader and if I don't hear any other nominations I'll declare the nominations closed and Colonel Bowie elected."

The crowd yelled and clapped and threw their odd assortment of hats in the air. "Three cheers for Colonel Bowie!" someone screamed, and the crowd roared, "Hip, hip, hooray!"

The speaker had left the box. There were several minutes of confusion. Then the crowd quieted again. Another man had mounted the box. He was a tall, broad-shouldered man with a heavy thatch of reddish hair, deep-set eyes, and a strong chin. There were shouts of "Hooray for old Jim Bowie!" He stood motionless on the box until the crowd was completely quiet.

"I must thank you, and I shall," he said, "but there are some other things I must say first. No man can be honest and say that praise does not warm his heart. Also, no man can be honest and fail to say the things that are true and right.

"First, your speaker said some unkind things regarding a people I love — the Mexican people. I have lived among them, married among them, and have had their sympathy in time of sorrow. I have worked with them and fought with them as companions in arms and found them honorable men. You must not forget that there are many Mexicans who feel as we do about the tyranny of Santa Anna and who are fighting at our side in a just cause.

"Next, regarding your selection of me as your leader. Let us not forget that Colonel Neill was entirely within his rights in his appointment of Colonel Travis as his successor. This is military procedure. And, it is true, it has been customary in the various battles we have had in Texas for the fighting men to select their own leaders in the field.

"One practice is perhaps just as right as the other, but it creates confusion. We are all fighting one cause and we must somehow find a procedure for doing it. While I promise you I will respect the honor you have extended me, I intend to go to Colonel Travis and ex-

plain your action. I will place myself at his disposal
to see what arrangements we can make that will keep
everyone happy and intent on the only end we serve —
God and Texas."

Bowie descended from the box and was gone. The
men stood in the square, cheering until their voices
were hoarse. Later, as the early evening fell, many
of them gathered in a hall where Mexican musicians
were playing for a fandango, or dance. Clumsy volunteer soldiers from Tennessee, Virginia, and New York
tried to dance the nimble Spanish steps with graceful
Mexican girls. Since there were not enough girls to
go around some of the men were awkwardly dancing
with each other.

When an intermission came there were cries for
David Crockett to make a speech.

Crockett stood on a box and joked with the crowd.
He had, he said, been asked how he had recruited
men for his company of volunteers.

"I'll tell you," he said, "it wasn't easy. But there was
this one young fellow I met, I could see he was of the
steamboat-and-alligator breed, and I asked him was
he a rhinoceros or a hyena, being so eager to fight the
Mexican invaders. And he says: 'Neither the one or
the other, Colonel, but a whole menagerie in myself.
I'm shaggy as a bear, wolfish about the head, active as

a cougar, and can grin like a hyena until the bark will curl off a gum log. There's a sprinkling of all sorts in me, from the lion down to the skunk. And before the war is over you'll pronounce me an entire zoological institute, or I miss a figure in my calculation. I promise to swallow Santa Anna without gagging, if you will only skewer back his ears and grease his head a little.' And that's the kind of fellows we was looking for and the kind of fellows we got."

The men roared with laughter, slapped each other on the back, and shook hands.

"So with men like that for company," Crockett continued, "I set out. But I made a farewell speech to my constituents, who had decided that, while I was a good fellow and the best squirrel shot for some miles around, they did not want me to serve them in Congress any more. I stood up, and in the most neighborly fashion I said: 'After due consideration I have decided that I am going to Texas and fight for liberty. You, my friends, can go plumb to hell!' "

When the laughter and cheering died Crockett took an old fiddle from the wall of the room and began scraping away with the bow, making outlandish sounds.

"Music!" the men shouted. "Johnny McGregor, get your pipes!"

A stocky young man appeared with bagpipes. He puffed and squeezed at the bag and fingered the pipes. There was no similarity between the tune from the pipes and the scraping sounds Crockett was getting from the fiddle. But the men stamped on the floor and clapped their hands. Some clasped hands and whirled around in a dance.

After a while they wearied. Crockett hung up the fiddle and McGregor, the bagpiper, leaned against a table, breathing hard from his work.

"Where's Willie?" someone shouted. "A song from Willie! Ah, there he is. Give us a song, Willie!"

A thin young man leaning against a wall smiled at

the shouting men. Then he threw back his head, and
as the room quieted he began singing in a sweet clear
voice.

"Oh Mary, oh Mary, 'twas for your sake alone,
I left my poor father and mother at home.
I left my poor father, my mother to roam —
I'm a troubled soldier, no friend and no home."

The young man paused. Someone in the room was
sniffling noisily. The young man continued.

"Adieu to old Kentucky I never more expect to see,
For love and misfortune has called me away,
For love and misfortune has called me to mourn,
I am a troubled soldier, no friend and no home."

6

The Alarm

THE VOLUNTEERS' ELECTION of Bowie as their leader provided the only real excitement there had been in San Antonio since the fighting in December.

Colonel Travis was in a difficult situation. He relied on Governor Smith as the source of his authority, and Smith was no more certain of his job as governor than Travis was of his as commandant. He wrote to Governor Smith: "My situation is truly awkward and delicate." And he told of the volunteers' action. He urged that more soldiers be sent to him as soon as possible.

But by the following day, Travis and Bowie had patched up their troubles and together sent a letter to Governor Smith, saying: "By an understanding of today Colonel J. Bowie has command of the volunteers of the garrison and Colonel W. B. Travis of the regulars and volunteer cavalry. All general orders and correspondence will henceforth be signed by both until Col. Neill's return."

So much for their differences. They also wrote: "From all the information we have received here, there is no doubt that the enemy will surely advance upon this place, and that this will be the first point of attack. We must, therefore, urge the necessity of sending reinforcements as speedily as possible . . ."

Neither Travis nor Bowie fully realized how right they were, nor how desperate their situation was becoming. For on the day they wrote, the Mexican army led by Santa Anna was in Laredo on the Rio Grande River, less than two hundred miles southwest of San Antonio.

As early as a month before, the men in San Antonio had heard that there were large movements of Mexican troops along the Rio Grande. But no one grasped the size of the force that soon was to be sent against them. No one seriously thought that Santa Anna would attempt to march against them in winter, when there was no food for the animals. They did not understand that this was a personal crusade on the part of Santa Anna. As a dictator he considered any opposition an affront to his own person. And he had long

since sworn to stamp out the independence movement
in Texas. But in the case of San Antonio de Bexar and
the Alamo it was worse. It was his brother-in-law,
General Martin Perfecto de Cos, who had been so
badly beaten there by the Texans in December, who
had been forced to surrender all arms and ammunition, retiring across the Rio Grande with a promise to
stay out of Texas thereafter. This sort of humiliation
Santa Anna could not stand, and he vowed to wipe
out all foreigners in Texas, to crush all resistance, and
— first of all — to destroy the little group of men who
were holding San Antonio de Bexar. General Cos, who
had promised the Texans he would withdraw beyond
the Rio Grande and stay there, was with him.

Santa Anna directed one comparatively small detachment of cavalry and infantry led by General Urrea
to Matamoros, the town at the mouth of the Rio
Grande. This column was then to swing north and
protect the right flank of Santa Anna's main force,
which then proceeded to march toward San Antonio.
This main force consisted of approximately 6000 men,
well armed, drilled, and equipped with horses and
mules.

The force was divided into brigades, and Santa
Anna, a somber-eyed man of alternate calm and vio-
lent temper, watched with satisfaction as they de-

parted from Laredo, a brigade at a time, on the hard march to San Antonio.

Unknown to the Mexican general and his troops, a young Mexican from San Antonio had been spying on their movements. The young man, named Blaz Herrera, was loyal to the Texas forces. He was a cousin of Captain John Seguin, a Mexican of San Antonio who was opposed to Santa Anna and was working closely with the Texans. When Blaz Herrera saw the army definitely preparing to move northward, he rode as fast as his horse could carry him and arrived, exhausted, in San Antonio on the night of February 18. He gave his news to Captain Seguin, who reported to the military authorities. Many of the Texan officers distrusted all Mexicans, even those who were faithfully trying to help them. And they refused to believe the report, thinking it might be a ruse to spread alarm.

But the Mexican population of San Antonio believed it. Throughout the nights and days that followed, family after family packed their household goods and, afoot or in wagons, deserted the town and headed for the country.

And Travis believed the report. He placed a sentry in the bell tower of the San Fernando cathedral, with instructions to toll the bell if he sighted troops advancing.

Some days later Santa Anna's army, after a desperately hard march, arrived at the Medina River, a few miles south of San Antonio. The forward troops were placed on the side of the river nearer San Antonio; the wagons and carts loaded with ammunition and supplies remained on the far side. A troop of cavalry was sent ahead to an elevation that protected Santa Anna's army from the view of San Antonio. By ascending the heights the cavalry troop could clearly see the town and observe any troop movements.

The young sentry in the church tower, his eyes aching from staring toward the south and west, caught a glimpse of color on the horizon. At first it seemed to be some brightly colored ribbons dancing in the breeze. Then the cavalrymen's lances appeared and then the cavalrymen themselves. He turned, grasped the bell rope and threw his weight on it, swinging free in the belfry. Overhead the great bronze bell turned slowly on its axle and then tolled out a deep-throated tone. The clapper swung and the bell tolled again and again.

Below, in Military Plaza and Constitution Plaza, the Texans stopped and stared toward the tower, shielding their eyes with their hands. Colonel Travis ran to the church, dashed up the stairs, then rapidly scaled the ladder to the bell tower.

The sentry was still swinging on the bell rope. Travis pulled him to one side. "What is it, lad? Where are they?"

The young man breathlessly pointed toward the south. Travis stared across the countryside and saw nothing.

The Mexican cavalry scouts had heard the bell tolling and, knowing that they had been seen, had quickly withdrawn behind the ridge of hills and were no longer visible.

Travis scolded the sentry for imagining things and returned to the plaza below. When his men asked what had happened he said it was nothing and went to his quarters.

Santa Anna's men continued to observe the Texans from places of concealment, and spies made their way into the town. They reported back to Santa Anna that the Texans considered the report a false alarm and were going ahead with plans for a fandango that night.

Santa Anna, knowing the Texans would be up late for the fandango, made plans for an attack early the next morning, when the Texans would be sleeping late after the party.

But during the night a heavy rain fell, and the Medina River rose rapidly. It was impossible to get the ammunition and supply wagons across the swollen stream. The attack had to be postponed.

7

The Siege Begins

ALTHOUGH TRAVIS had been unable to see the patrol
the sentry had seen and although he had reassured
his men that it was a false alarm, he was, nevertheless,
convinced that Santa Anna's forces were not far away.
He called for volunteers to ride out to see what they
could find. He chose two men who still had their
horses with them in San Antonio—Dr. John Sutherland and John W. Smith.

Dr. Sutherland, a Virginian, had been in San Antonio for the past month, helping to care for the sick
and wounded in the Alamo garrison. Smith was also
a Virginian but he had lived in San Antonio for almost
six years, had fought with the Texas forces against
General Cos the previous December, and was well

acquainted with the countryside around San Antonio.

The two men set out on the Laredo road, and the sentry in the San Fernando bell tower was cautioned to observe their movements and to ring the bell if they turned and rode back toward San Antonio at a run.

Sutherland and Smith reached Prospect Hill, no more than two miles from San Antonio. They cautiously rode up the slope and, reaching the ridge, looked down on the other side. There, less than one hundred and fifty yards from them, were Santa Anna's cavalrymen, mounted and lined up in parade formation. An officer rode up and down in front of the line, waving his sword and giving orders.

The two scouts turned their horses and, once they were well protected from view by the crest of the hill, urged them into a gallop. Sutherland's horse was unshod. It slipped in the wet clay and fell, pinning one of Sutherland's legs beneath it. Smith reined his horse, dismounted, and returned to help his companion. He got the horse to its feet and then assisted Sutherland back into the saddle.

The sentry in the church tower had been watching them, and now the bell began to toll again. This time the Texans believed the report. They briskly started for the Alamo. Inside the fortress everyone worked feverishly. Men who had done little but loaf for a

month now turned to and worked mightily, packing earth against the walls to strengthen them, piling sandbags, rolling artillery pieces into place, building platforms inside the walls from which riflemen could see to fire.

The scouts, Sutherland and Smith, rode into the main enclosure of the Alamo. David Crockett hailed them. "Come on," he shouted, "Colonel Travis is waiting to hear from you."

Travis was seated at a table in a barracks room, a blank sheet of paper in front of him, a quill pen in his hand.

The two scouts quickly told their story. They estimated the number of cavalrymen they had seen at between 1200 and 1500 — almost ten times the number of effective men the Texans had in the Alamo.

Travis' hand raced across the paper, writing a message for the people of Gonzales, the nearest Texas settlement. He wrote:

> The enemy in large force is in sight. We want men and provisions. Send them to us. We have 150 men and are determined to defend the Alamo to the last. Give us assistance.
>
> W. B. TRAVIS, Col. Commanding.
>
> P.S. Send an express to San Felipe with news, night and day.

He looked up at the two scouts.

"Will your injured leg permit you to ride to Gonzales with this, Dr. Sutherland?"

"Yes, sir," said Sutherland. Limping heavily, he walked out, followed by Smith. Their horses were still lathered from the last hard ride. They led them out of the Alamo and mounted and rode east toward Gonzales. Behind them they could now plainly see Santa Anna's troops riding into San Antonio.

Crockett remained with Travis.

"Here I am, Colonel," said Crockett. "Assign me to some place."

"What rank would you like as an officer?" Travis asked.

"Let's say that I am a sort of high private," said Crockett. "Just assign me some place and I and my Tennessee boys will defend it, all right."

Travis thanked him and asked him to assume, with his company, the defense of a picket-and-earth wall that connected the Alamo chapel with the high thick wall that enclosed the main court. It was the weakest point in the entire fortification.

Crockett agreed and went outside to rejoin his men.

"My boys," said Crockett, "the Colonel had paid us a great compliment. He has given us to defend the weakest, most tender point in this whole sorry fortress."

"Is that a compliment?" asked one of the men.

"Who else but Tennessee men could be trusted in such a place?" asked Crockett. "It is a compliment indeed, and a tribute to the stout hearts and sharp eyes of Tennessee men."

"But, Colonel," said one of the youngest, "I ain't a Tennessee man. I'm from Georgia and I ain't seventeen yet."

"You're a Tennessee man now, lad," said Crockett, and slapped the young man on the shoulder. "Now would you look what's goin' on over there." He pointed toward the town. A red flag was being hoisted to the San Fernando cathedral tower.

"What does that mean, Colonel?"

"That there, sonny, is the 'no quarter' flag. No nonsense, no mercy, no way out."

And as he said it the men of the Alamo replied. Their eighteen-pounder, the largest weapon they had, roared and sent a cannon ball whistling into the center of San Antonio de Bexar. The men in the Alamo cheered and gathered on the walls to stare into the place they had just left — for ever.

"Victory or death!" someone shouted, and then all the men took up the cry: "Victory or death!"

The thirteen-day siege of the Alamo had begun. It was February 23, 1836.

8

Return of a Courier

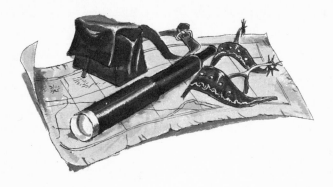

THE FIRST SHOT fired from the Alamo was soon answered by Mexican artillery, but it did little damage. The balls would strike the thick walls, chip some of the stones — and occasionally the flying chips would strike the men inside the fortress. But the men proceeded with their duties as though nothing were happening.

When they left San Antonio they had driven before them any stray cattle they found in the streets. Thirty head of cattle were now herded into the small corral at the back of the Alamo — a supply of meat. When the cattle were killed the raw hides would be packed with earth and used to strengthen the barricades.

Before entering the fortress the men had prowled through the Mexican huts that surrounded the Alamo to make certain none of Santa Anna's men were hiding. The huts were deserted, but the men found ninety bushels of corn, which they carried inside the fortress.

In the center of the main court of the Alamo a group of men were digging. Some were already out of sight below ground, passing loosened dirt and stones up to the men above, who carried them off to the sides to build elevated platforms so that the artillery pieces could shoot over the walls. But this was not the main purpose of the digging: it was for a well. The Alamo received its water supply through two irrigation ditches running under the wall. The Texans knew that as soon as possible the Mexicans outside would cut off the water supply by blocking the ditches, both of which were fed by the little San Antonio River.

Travis was standing in the center of the main court. He shouted for attention. The men halted their work and looked at him. With his sword he gestured toward the ruins of the church tower. A large pole with a lanyard attached had been raised from the tower, and now a flag was being raised. It was like the Mexican flag, with vertical red, white, and green bands, except that in the white band, where the Mexican flag carried the national insignia, this had in heavy bold print

"1824." This was the only flag the Texans had. It was a reminder of their demand for return to the Mexican constitution of 1824, the constitution that had given them rights and liberties Santa Anna had later taken away.

The men stood silently for a minute watching the flag, and then returned to their work.

There was a shout from the church tower, where a lookout had been posted. Men scrambled up the walls to see what was happening. From the east they could see a man riding his horse at a full run. As he neared, the gates were unbarred, while men stood nearby with rifles ready in case it was a ruse.

The horse, a big cream-colored animal lathered white, pounded into the court.

"Bonham!" the men shouted, and crowded around him, Travis among them. "What's the news?" they cried. "Are they coming? Are they coming?"

Lieutenant James Butler Bonham was a tall dark man with an olive skin and flashing black eyes. He had returned from Goliad, where he had been sent to seek help from the only other Texas garrison, commanded by Colonel James Walker Fannin.

Bonham brushed his clothing, caught his breath, and said to Travis, "I wish I had good word. I do not. Colonel Fannin says that he can give us neither men

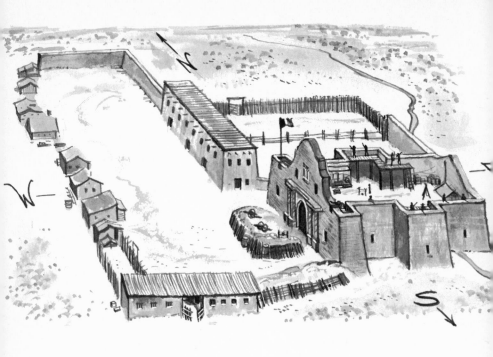

nor equipment. He is busy with strengthening Goliad
and says he can spare nothing."

Travis' face darkened. "Does he understand our
position? Does he know the strength of the enemy
we are facing?"

Bonham shrugged. "He knows only that a Mexican
force has been sent toward Bexar."

"A Mexican force," Travis roared. "*The* Mexican
force. Santa Anna himself may be out there." He
gestured toward the west. "And they are receiving
reinforcements by the hour. We will be outnumbered
by forty, perhaps fifty to one."

"He did not know that," Bonham said. "He could

not know it. I did not know it myself until this moment."

"True," Travis sighed. "But what has become of
his expedition against Matamoros?"

"He has word that General Urrea is in Matamoros
with a strong force and is preparing to march against
Goliad. So he is preparing Goliad. He has at least
three times the number of men that we have here."

Travis shook his head. "Come inside and rest." The
two men walked away together.

Of all the men at the Alamo there were no two
so alike as were Travis and Bonham. Both were South
Carolinians; both were men of high principles and
hot tempers — and neither had any trace of fear.

They had gone to a small country school together
in South Carolina. When Travis' family moved to
Alabama he corresponded with Bonham, and continued to do so until they met again in Texas, where
Travis had gone in 1831. He practiced law, became
involved in a quarrel with the local Mexican commandant, later organized a small group of volunteers
and captured a garrison of Mexicans. General Cos
put a price on his head, but it did not stop Travis.
He joined the army that was later to drive Cos out of
Texas, and while serving as a scout he captured 200
Mexicans. He was a close friend of the Governor,

Henry Smith, and at Smith's request he operated a recruiting office for the Texas army in San Felipe de Austin, until ordered to San Antonio. He was generally regarded as the one man most responsible for the Texans' rebellion against Mexico.

Bonham was a rebel, too. In college he had organized a revolt because of bad food and was expelled. Later, when practicing law, he once gave a beating to a rival lawyer for an insult to a lady, and when the judge objected Bonham offered to whip him also. He was sentenced to jail, but his gallant behavior had caused such an impression that ladies of the town brought him flowers and fine foods daily. When he followed his friend Travis to Texas, in 1835, it was only natural that he would become involved in the revolution. He joined Travis in the recruiting office, became a lieutenant in the cavalry, and was one of Travis' most trusted couriers at the Alamo.

9

The Burning of the Huts

THE MEXICAN BOMBARDMENT of the Alamo continued, but it did little harm and the men in the Alamo began to joke about it.

Travis, meanwhile, knew how grim the situation was. Mexican reinforcements were arriving, and the Alamo was getting none. Supplies, particularly of ammunition, were limited. Every shot must be made to count.

Travis tried to convey the seriousness of his position in a series of messages that he sent by courier to other Texas settlements. The nearest ones were Gonzales, sixty-four miles due east, and Goliad, sixty miles south of Gonzales. There was no central government to which they could report. Governor Smith was in San Felipe de Austin, but whether he held authority as governor was in some doubt. In the meantime, Travis tried to get word of the Alamo's plight to as many Texans as possible, in the faint hope that some help might come from some place.

On the second day of the siege he wrote:

> Commandancy of the Alamo
> Bexar, F'by 24th, 1836
>
> To the People of Texas & All Americans in the world:
>
> Fellow Citizens and Compatriots — I am besieged by a thousand or more of the Mexicans under Santa Anna. I have sustained a continual Bombardment and cannonade for 24 hours and have not lost a man. The enemy has demanded a surrender at discretion, otherwise, the garrison are to be put to the sword, if the fort is taken. I have answered the demand with a cannon shot, and our flag still waves proudly from the walls. *I shall never surrender or retreat.* Then, I call upon you in the name of Liberty, of patriotism, and everything dear to the American character, to come to our aid with all dispatch. The enemy is receiving reinforcements daily and will no doubt increase to three or four thousand in four or five days. If this call is neglected, I am determined to sustain myself

as long as possible and die like a soldier who
never forgets what is due to his own honor and
that of his country. VICTORY OR DEATH.

WILLIAM BARRET TRAVIS
Lt. Col. Comdt.

Jim Bowie, who was to have shared the command
with Travis, had fallen ill with pneumonia. He lay
on a cot in the section of the barracks that had been
designated as a hospital. He begged Travis to take
full command and ordered his followers to obey
Travis as they would him. At times he became deliri-
ous with fever, but insisted at all times that his two
pistols be beside him on the cot. His knife was still

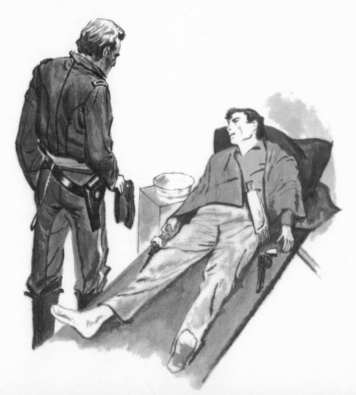

strapped to his side, a knife with which he had won many fights. Now, all over Texas, men carried similar weapons, which they called bowie knives.

During the second day a company of Mexicans crossed the San Antonio River well to the south of the Alamo and stealthily approached the fortress, hiding behind the abandoned Mexican huts, or *jacals*.

The Texans watched the movement with interest, and the frontiersmen with their long rifles picked off the Mexicans, one by one, as they exposed themselves. Their aim was deadly. One Mexican who survived the battle said long afterward: "When the Texan devils had you in the sights you were dead, even before the trigger was pulled."

Travis observed the action, and although he was proud of his men's marksmanship he was also worried. A small enemy movement among the huts could be controlled by rifle fire; but if a large body of men adopted the same tactics, using the shacks for shelter, the rifle fire would not be so effective.

Late in the afternoon he ordered an assembly in the main court of all who were not on lookout duty or manning walls. He explained the danger and said: "I would like two volunteers, young men who are fast on their feet, who will go out under the cover of darkness and set fire to all of these buildings. We need a clear field of action before us, one in which nothing is concealed. Who will volunteer?"

Charles Despallier, a young man from Louisiana who spoke with a strong French accent, stepped forward. "I will be proud to go, sir." A second young man, Robert Brown, joined him. "I'll go, sir."

"Good," said Travis, and walked with the two of them to the south wall. He pointed to the huts. "If we had plenty of gunpowder we could knock them to pieces with artillery. But we do not. Fire is the only answer, and it will be difficult. To run from the fortress with flaming torches would be suicide. You would be shot in a moment. You must devise some way of setting fire and returning safely to the Alamo. I leave it to you."

"I think I have a plan," said Despallier. "Come with me."

In the barracks they found some old candle stubs, too short for use. They cut them even shorter, trimming the wicks so they would light easily. They prepared two dozen, one for each *jacal*.

When the sun had gone down they made their final preparations. They went to the corral behind the Alamo and took several armloads of hay, stuffing it into cloth bags. Each had a flint and steel and wads of tinder, and a package of fat pine splinters.

They had memorized the location of the huts. Despallier was to take those on the right side of the path, Brown those on the left.

As soon as it was completely dark the two young men stole out of the rear of the Alamo, lowering themselves into the corral and then climbing the corral fence. They kept close to the wall and walked quietly to the corner of the church. Here they threw themselves flat on the ground and crept forward. The ground had been plowed up by the Mexican artillery balls, and this helped. They would pause to rest in low places, then creep forward again.

Intermittently there would be the crack of rifle

fire from the Mexican camp as they crept along the
ground, shivering in the north wind. Occasionally
the wind would carry snatches of men's talk from the
Alamo.

Finally Despallier and Brown came to the cluster
of huts and divided them, each taking an equal
number. They would enter a hut and make a pile
within it of broken pieces of furniture, scraps of fire-
wood, dead grass, and the hay they carried with them.
They would strike a fire with their flint and steel, light
a candle stub and place it at the base of the heap,
making certain first that the draft would push the
flames toward the kindling rather than away. Then
they would move on to the next hut and repeat the
process, always looking back to make certain the

previous buildings were not aflame yet. The first sight of a blazing building would, they knew, bring rifle fire from the Mexicans.

Finally they reached the end of the line. Brown, unable to see in the dark after facing a lighted candle, stumbled on something on the ground. He gasped. "Oh — it's you, Charlie. You had me right scared there for a minute. You finish yours?"

"Yes," whispered Despallier. "And look!"

They could see flames inside the farthest shack.

"Now we hurry," Despallier said, no longer bothering to lower his voice. He struck a spark with his flint, lighted his last candle stub, and placed it under a wad of hay at the side of the last building. The north wind spread the flames and the two young men jumped to their feet and ran as hard as they could for the gate in the south wall of the Alamo. They could be seen now in the light of the fire. There were several rifle shots, and they heard rifle balls whistling over their heads as they ran. There were answering rifle shots from the walls of the Alamo, and the gate swung open for them to dash inside.

Together they mounted one of the platforms built inside the walls. From here they could see the lines of blazing huts. David Crockett was beside them.

"Two of the best Tennessee firebugs ever I see

didn't come from Tennessee," he said. "Maybe this will give old Santy Anny an idea what's in store for him someday."

Much later in the night Travis was again sitting at his table, composing another dispatch.

> I take [he wrote] great pleasure in stating that both officers and men conducted themselves with firmness and bravely. . . . Charles Despallier and Robert Brown gallantly sallied out and set fire to the houses which afforded the enemy shelter, in the face of enemy fire. Indeed, the whole of the men who were brought into action, conducted themselves with such undaunted heroism that it might be an injustice to discriminate. The Hon. David Crockett was seen at all points, animating the men to do their duty. I have every reason to apprehend an attack . . . very soon; but I shall hold out to the last extremity, hoping to secure reinforcements in a day or two. Do hasten on aid to me as rapidly as possible, as from the superior number of the enemy, it will be impossible for us to keep them out much longer . . . If they overpower us, we fall a sacrifice at the shrine of our country, and we hope posterity and our country will do our memory justice. Give me help, oh my Country! Victory or Death!

10

Another Mission

It is DOUBTFUL that any of the men in the Alamo realized how totally hopeless their position was. Even Travis still entertained some hope that help would come.

There were only two men in Texas who might have come to their aid. One was James Walker Fannin, who had at Goliad a force of about 500 men, or more than three times the number besieged in the Alamo. The other was Sam Houston, who had been — and might still be, no one knew for certain — commander-in-chief of Texas' almost nonexistent army. And Houston's whereabouts at the moment was a mystery.

Fannin, the commander at Goliad, was one of the few men in Texas who had had any formal military training. He had been a student at the military academy at West Point for eighteen months, until expelled for fighting. More recently he had been engaged in slave-trading in Texas, which was contrary to Mexican law.

He had been active in the campaign against General Cos at San Antonio, and was a leader in the plans for an expedition against Matamoros. Sam Houston opposed the Matamoros expedition, and since he could not control his subordinates and there was no government to back up his authority, he had shrugged his shoulders, asked for a furlough, and disappeared.

But the Matamoros expedition was doomed to failure. The Mexican detachment under General Urrea which Santa Anna had sent to Matamoros from Laredo had cooled the Texans' enthusiasm for the adventure. Only a few foolhardy parties set out for Matamoros. The bulk of the force remained at Goliad with Fannin, who, in the absence of Houston, was now the highest-ranking officer the Texans had.

Goliad was close to the Gulf of Mexico and could control shipping through Aransas Pass and Matagorda Bay. With these points controlled, Mexico would have difficulty shipping supplies to her troops in Texas.

Fannin knew that General Cos the year before had relied on shipping for his supplies of food and ammunition. The Texans cut his supply lines; this had as much to do with the defeat of Cos at San Antonio as did the brave assault by Ben Milam and his men. Fannin believed that control of Goliad might similarly help to defeat Santa Anna.

But Santa Anna knew this as well as Fannin. Consequently he was not depending on shipping but was instead bringing his supplies overland.

Fannin kept his men occupied with rebuilding and strengthening the fortress at Goliad. Like the Alamo, it had once been a mission, but Fannin and his men renamed it Fort Defiance. They rebuilt the walls, dug ditches for a water supply, built platforms for artillery pieces and riflemen. They were well supplied with food and ammunition but were short on cannon and horses.

Travis had sent numerous couriers to Fannin with pleas for assistance, among them Bonham. But Fannin had steadfastly insisted that what he was doing at Goliad was more important.

Early in the morning of the fifth day of the siege, Travis called his old friend Bonham to him again. Travis sat sprawled on a straw mattress, leaning against the stone wall of the barracks. His face was blackened from the cannon that he had been firing from the north wall. He had unbuckled his sword and it lay at his side. He had slipped off his boots. It was the first time since the beginning of the siege that Bonham had seen Travis in such disarray, and he knew Travis permitted it only because they were old friends.

Travis' voice was weary. "For the moment we are not colonel and lieutenant. We are two men who have known each other for a long time. As an old friend and companion in arms, would you be willing to make another trip as a courier? It becomes increasingly difficult, as I am sure you know."

"Of course," said Bonham.

"I must at all cost do two things. I must get word to the Texas settlements of our plight here and keep them informed of the progress of the siege. I must let them know that Texas, without a government, without an army worthy of the name, still has some brave men who are fighting.

"In a few days' time representatives of all the colonies will meet in Washington-on-the-Brazos to form a government. The men who meet there must know what we are doing for them, and it may speed their actions. The colonies must know, must be persuaded to send men and supplies to our aid. If you carry this word to Gonzales, the good people there will see that it is sent on.

"And I wish you to go to Colonel Fannin at Goliad and impress upon him once more the urgency of our position, our frightful need of the assistance that only he can supply. If Texas has an army it is the five hundred men whom Fannin commands. They must come. Tell him that."

"Where shall I go first, to Gonzales or to Goliad?" Bonham asked.

"First to Goliad and Fannin. That is of the greatest urgency. Then go to Gonzales. Tell them to send word to Washington-on-the-Brazos, and urge them to raise some volunteers. And tell them to bring their own gunpowder."

It would be an hour more before full daylight. Bonham cautiously led his big cream-colored horse out of the corral at the rear of the Alamo. He draped a dark homespun blanket over the horse's back and neck to make him less visible. Leading the horse, Bonham walked slightly ahead, shuffling his feet along the ground, feeling for stones that might make a noise if struck with the horse's hoofs.

It was deathly quiet and the night was dark. The horse's breathing sounded deafeningly loud. He crossed one of the irrigation ditches that supplied the Alamo with water and began ascending a slope toward the east. Far to the right Bonham could see the faint

flicker of a campfire; and the eastern horizon was beginning to turn a pale gray. He walked a mile or more. The campfire he had seen was behind him now. Bonham swung the blanket off the horse; but just as he prepared to mount he heard the pounding of horses' hoofs. Looking back he could dimly see two horsemen carrying lances riding toward him at a run. He threw himself into the saddle and kicked his horse into a run. His rifle was ready if he had to shoot it out, and as he rode he looked back over his shoulders. Gradually the two Mexicans fell back and when the full sun was over the horizon Bonham was safely away on his last mission.

11

Sam Houston

THE OTHER MAN who might have helped Travis and his followers at the Alamo was Sam Houston. And no one knew exactly where Sam Houston was.

Almost everything about Sam Houston had been a mystery since he appeared on the Texas scene, but everyone was aware of him. He was far taller than the average man — a head taller than most. He dressed in colorful clothing and usually wore an Indian blanket draped around his shoulders. He had a great, booming voice, and spoke with eloquence. He was a natural leader of men, yet in some ways he seemed to want to avoid leading them.

When he had arrived in Texas a few years before, he had come from Indian territory to the north, traveling alone. A few people among the Texas colonists knew something of his background.

"Each time Sam Houston has troubles," they said, "he runs off with the Indians." And they told this story: that when he was a boy living in Tennessee he ran away from home after some sort of scrape and went to live with a tribe of Cherokee Indians nearby, learning their language, living and dressing as Indians do. Sometime later he enlisted in the United States Army and served with distinction under General Andrew Jackson, now President of the United States, in the wars against the Creek Indians.

After the war he became a lawyer in Tennessee, a leader of the Tennessee militia, a Congressman and, finally, Governor of Tennessee. But suddenly he left the governorship of Tennessee and disappeared into the wilderness across the Mississippi. He had gone, it was learned later, to live among his old friends the Cherokees, whom the United States government was pushing farther and farther west.

He lived among the Cherokees for six years before settling in Texas. He had, in the meantime, become an agent for the Cherokees, and sometimes went to Washington in their behalf and spoke with his old friend, President Jackson.

It was not clear, in Texas, whether he had come

there as a representative of the Cherokee nation or something else. During his first trip he held some parleys with the Comanche Indians near San Antonio; this may have been done as a representative of the Cherokees, or merely as a man who was interested in Indians.

Or, the gossip ran, he may have been a representative of President Andrew Jackson. Everyone believed that Jackson wanted Texas to win her independence from Mexico and join the United States, but for diplomatic reasons he could do nothing about it openly.

Or he may have been a representative of one of the many Eastern land companies that were speculating in Texas real estate.

Or he may have come solely as an adventurer.

Since many of the men who were coming to Texas in those days were fugitives from justice elsewhere, it was considered impolite to inquire too closely into their reasons for being there.

Houston set himself up as a lawyer in Nacogdoches and almost immediately became a public figure. He at first associated himself with the more moderate faction — the "peace party," which wanted nothing more than a return to the guarantees of the Mexican constitution of 1824, as opposed to the "war party," which wanted an outright break with Mexico and

complete independence. Later he was to become an advocate of outright independence.

He was elected a delegate to "the consultation," a meeting of representatives of all the Texan colonists held in San Felipe de Austin in October and November, 1835, which set up a temporary government of Texas. Henry Smith was elected Governor, and Sam Houston was chosen commander-in-chief of the Texas army — with the provision that he should raise troops for a regular army but that he was not in charge of the volunteer troops already fighting General Martin Perfecto de Cos at San Antonio.

Houston's command was far from complete. He

was opposed to the Matamoros expedition but he could not enforce his views, since he had no control over volunteers.

After the defeat of General Cos he ordered the garrison in the Alamo to withdraw to a safer position and destroy the fortification there. This order, too, was ignored. There was no stable government to back up his orders.

A constitutional convention had been called for March 1, 1836. Houston knew that until it met there could be nothing like a firm governmental or military authority. He took a furlough and, as he had done so often in the past, disappeared.

He went among his old friends the Cherokees. One group of the Cherokee nation, despairing of the broken promises of the United States, had migrated into eastern Texas. They were led by two war lords, Chief Bowles (or "The Bowl") and Big Mush. They had begun to negotiate with the Mexican government for rights to settle there permanently. It was known that since the beginning of trouble with Texas Santa Anna had sent agents among them. If the Indians would help the Mexicans put down the Texas rebels they would be rewarded with permanent grants of land. Although it was not generally known by the Texas colonists, this could have been a grave danger.

Houston was peculiarly fitted to meet the problem. He knew both The Bowl and Big Mush from his years of living among their people.

Traveling alone, he went to their settlement in eastern Texas, renewed his friendships with them, exchanged gifts, and began a series of parleys with them in their own language. In the Cherokee tongue Houston was known as "The Raven." Houston knew the Indian ways and was in no rush to achieve his ends. But finally after several weeks of negotiation he reached an agreement with them on February 23, 1836, the first day of the siege of the Alamo. In return for remaining neutral in the conflict with Mexico he, The Raven, would see that Texas gave them permanent "rights of domicile and tillage."

(It should be noted that after the war with Mexico the Texas senate refused to ratify this treaty. Subsequently the Cherokees were bloodily driven out of Texas and back into Indian territory, both The Bowl and Big Mush being killed on Texas soil.)

Having achieved his goal, Houston started for Washington-on-the-Brazos where he was to be a delegate to the constitutional convention.

12

No Help from Fannin

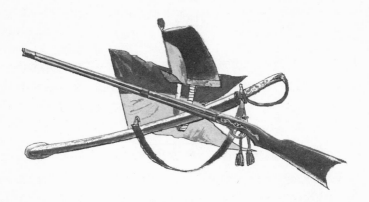

Bᴏɴʜᴀᴍ ʀᴏᴅᴇ his horse as hard as he dared across the rough country, following the southeastward course of the San Antonio River. He hoped that he might reach his destination on the second night, but the weary horse slowed to a stop some miles short of Goliad, and Bonham slept by the riverside.

The next morning he rode on toward Goliad, which was plainly in view, situated on a rocky elevation above the river. As he approached the town he could see a large group of soldiers outside the gates of Fort Defiance. At last, Bonham thought, Fannin is sending us some reinforcements. He spurred the tired horse ahead. But as he approached the settlement his face grew longer. The soldiers were not leaving Fort

Defiance. They were entering it.

Bonham rode into the enclosure. The soldiers he
had seen were weary and mudstained. They were
busily taking equipment back inside the fortress. One
cartload of supplies was being drawn by a team of
oxen; another was being pulled in by the men
themselves.

Bonham dismounted, strode across the courtyard,
and entered the barracks room that served Fannin as
his office. Fannin looked haggard and dirty. He sat
with one leg extended while an orderly cleaned the
mud from his boots.

"Compliments of Colonel Travis, sir," said Bonham.

"Good morning, Bonham," said Fannin. "Please be seated. What is the news of my friend Travis?"

"The same, sir, only worse. You have had the dispatches, I take it, on the arrival of the enemy. The Mexicans receive reinforcements daily, heavier reinforcements each day. We estimate that there is a total effective force of six thousand men opposing us, led, we think, by General Santa Anna personally. Our garrison consists of no more than a hundred and fifty men. We have forty pieces of artillery but we cannot mount more than half because of our shortage of powder, and those pieces that are mounted we can employ only in the greatest emergency, for the same reason. We are in desperate need of both men and supplies — mainly rifle and cannon powder. Since we have so little time for eating, our food supply is adequate. Of water we have plenty."

Fannin listened solemnly. One hand busily twisted one of the brass buttons on his tunic.

"And of the effective men you have," he said, finally, "I take it that most of them are volunteers — that you have very few regular soldiers."

"Correct, sir," said Bonham, and his face reddened as he said it. "But with all respect, I should like to point out that without the volunteers we would have been lost before now. When honest, freedom-loving men are in a fight, sir, it is impossible to tell the regular soldiers from the volunteer."

"I meant no offense, Lieutenant," said Fannin. "My men here at Fort Defiance — I have, you see, given this presidio a good American-sounding name — almost all my men are volunteers, and they elected me their colonel. They recognize the fact that I have had formal training as a soldier and have been educated in military matters — an advantage few of them enjoy.

"No, I meant no disrespect. And I wish that I could be of assistance to my friend Travis. As it happens, I started out with three hundred and twenty men bound for Bexar only yesterday, but we turned back."

"What happened, sir?"

"We were scarcely two miles out of Goliad when one of our supply wagons broke down. While we were attempting to repair it the oxen wandered off. There was such a great delay that after talking with members of my staff I decided we would best serve the cause of Texas by returning here and continuing to strengthen our fortress.

"What you have told me convinces me that this decision was correct. By the time we could have reached the Alamo it would have been too late and it would have been a useless sacrifice of good troops."

"But, sir —"

Fannin held up his hand. "I know what you are going to say, Lieutenant, but allow me, for a moment, to speak as a brother officer rather than a superior. Let us be realistic.

"Travis' position is impossible. Hopeless. He certainly could not hold out until I could get there with a significant number of troops. And I very seriously doubt that he can hold out for the shorter time it will take you to return there.

"There are times in the life of an officer when he must be guided by consideration of maximum effectiveness. To be blunt, it would be foolish for you to return. The Alamo is lost, and our good friends with it, unless they can either withdraw successfully or arrange honorable terms with this Mexican villain, Santa Anna, which I doubt. Travis is your friend. He may have meant this mission as a way to save your life.

"I urge you to stay here with me. I can well use a man of your spirit and determination on my staff. Remember, we are on the main channel of supply here; General Urrea will within a matter of days attack us, and if Goliad and Fort Defiance fall the colonies are defenseless. I urge you to remain with us.

I could, as the senior officer in the field, order it, but I prefer to leave it to your good judgment."

Bonham arose. "Is there nothing I can say to change your mind, sir? No reason I can use — either military or humane? No reassurance I can give Colonel Travis?"

"I've expressed my honest opinion, Lieutenant, and have given you my most sincere advice. Let me say that I shall make every effort to send aid; if it appears that the Mexicans are changing their strategy and that Fort Defiance is no longer threatened, then I shall dispatch reinforcements at once. Tell Travis that. But at present this appears unlikely."

"Then, sir, with your permission I will be on my way." Bonham walked out.

13

The Thirty-two from Gonzales

AFTER HIS disappointing conversation with Fannin, Bonham stayed overnight at Goliad. He was anxious to be on the way, but he had to give his horse some rest—and there were no horses in Goliad that he could trade for. The next morning at dawn he started north for Gonzales, his last hope of getting reinforcements for his friends at the Alamo.

Gonzales was to the Texas revolution what Lexington was to the War of Independence. This was where the revolution had really started.

Four years earlier the Mexican garrison at the Alamo had given the people of Gonzales a small cannon for use in helping to defend themselves against the Indians who had been burning houses and destroying crops. The cannon was small, old, and virtually useless; furthermore, there were no cannon balls or powder to go with it. The men of Gonzales went right on fighting Indians with their rifles as they had before.

In the autumn of 1835 the Mexican government had ordered all Texas colonists disarmed. A corporal and a squad of soldiers were sent to reclaim the cannon from Gonzales. When the Mexican soldiers demanded the cannon the people of Gonzales threw them into the town jail. Until then they hadn't thought much about the useless cannon. It now became a symbol of resistance that might, if surrendered to the Mexicans, in time be used against them.

The cannon was buried in a peach orchard for safekeeping, and the people of Gonzales prepared for the retaliation they knew would come.

Among the preparations was the making of the first Texas flag—made from an old white silk wedding dress. The flag bore a picture of the cannon and the motto: "Come and Take It."

The Mexicans next sent a lieutenant and a hundred dragoons to do what the corporal and his squad had failed to do. The Mexican soldiers halted on the west bank of the Guadalupe River, about four miles from Gonzales, apparently trying to determine a course of action. While they hesitated, the men of Gonzales attacked, armed with long-barreled flintlock rifles and lances made with ground-down files mounted on saplings. Too, they had dug up the cannon from the peach orchard, had mounted it on a wooden cart with wheels sawed from sections of a tree trunk, and it was drawn slowly by a team of oxen. It was loaded with a charge of chains, nails, bolts, hinges — any scrap iron that could be found — and might have done heavy damage if it had been fired. But it was never necessary to fire it. At the sight of the men of Gonzales the Mexican soldiers turned and fled. Meanwhile the wooden wheels of the gun carriage caught fire from friction and it was finally abandoned in a creek bottom.

Gonzales then had become a rallying point for the

volunteers who later attacked and defeated General Cos in San Antonio. It was the last outpost of Anglo-American Texas before reaching the Mexican Texas of San Antonio. It was a communications center; news of the fighting at San Antonio was always relayed to the other colonies by way of Gonzales. Gonzales had been generous in providing volunteers — there were many Gonzales men in the Alamo — and it was a point at which other volunteers would gather.

Bonham based his hope on this, but as he rode into the town he could not see a single man. There were women and children moving about, but no men.

He rode directly to the home of Andrew Ponton, the *alcalde*, or mayor of the colony. Ponton's house was like the others in the town — two log cabins joined together by a single roof. Ponton, a small, white-haired man, met him at the door and invited him in. He and his wife were sitting at a table in front of the hearth.

"Please eat with us," said Ponton. "But I must warn you that there is little choice. We have," and he gestured at the table, "some corn bread, onions, and clabber. There is no meat. All in the town have given their dried and cured meat to the volunteers and there has been no time either to butcher or kill game. And very few men to do it."

"Food is not my concern," said Bonham, holding up his hand. "We need men and gunpowder at the Alamo."

"Did you come direct from the Alamo?" asked Ponton.

"No," said Bonham. "I left the Alamo on Saturday and have been to Goliad. I came here from there. Fannin is not sending us the reinforcements we had hoped for."

"Yes, I had feared that," said Ponton.

"Do you have reinforcements for us here?" Bonham asked.

"That is why I asked if you had come direct from the Alamo," said Ponton. "If you had, you might well have passed our men on the road."

"How many?" Bonham asked, his face brightening.

"There are thirty-two men," said Ponton, and he watched as Bonham's smile faded.

"Only thirty-two?"

"They are the last of the Gonzales volunteers, my son. There is hardly an able-bodied man left in the settlement. Only a few of us old men to look out for the women and children. It is the last thing we can offer Colonel Travis. We have no more men, no more rifles, no more gunpowder. They left on Sunday.

They should by now be in the Alamo fighting side by side with your comrades.

"We have, of course, forwarded all messages to Washington-on-the-Brazos. The convention opened there yesterday and, God willing, will declare the independence of Texas, adopt a constitution, and form a government. And, most important at the moment, organize an army that can come to the aid of the brave men who are fighting at the Alamo. But I doubt that it will be in time."

Bonham seemed not to be listening. "Only thirty-two men," he said. "Why, that can make no difference at all against six thousand."

"No difference at all," said Ponton. "We have had two dispatches since you left, and the situation grows more grave by the hour. All of our thirty-two men knew, I am sure, that they were marching to certain death. I think it may by this time be useless for you to return. If you would accept a suggestion, you might well ride to Washington-on-the-Brazos and appear before the delegates there as a man who has been in the Alamo, who has seen the fighting, who has seen the great odds against our men. This might inspire them to move with speed and decisiveness, and you might in that way serve a greater end than returning to your death."

Bonham shook his head slowly.

Ponton sighed. "I knew it would be useless to try to dissuade you."

"Thank you, sir," said Bonham, "for your understanding. With the support and blessing of good people such as yourself and the townspeople of Gonzales, we cannot fail."

Bonham strode from the house, mounted his horse, and started toward the west as fast as the tired horse would carry him.

14

A Mexican Assault

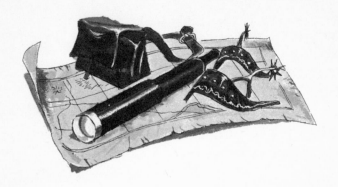

Bᴏɴʜᴀᴍ, on his mission to Goliad and Gonzales, was conscious of the passage of time, of one day following another.

His comrades in the Alamo were not. Although darkness followed daylight again and again, none was conscious of where one day ended and another began. There was never time to go to the cornshuck mattresses that served as beds — except for the wounded or the very ill, such as Jim Bowie, a dying man. He roused himself only long enough to urge the men, who were fiercely loyal to him, to give their loyalty in like measure to Colonel Travis. Then he would fall back on his bed, his weapons near at hand.

His companions, if they slept at all, did so leaning

against the walls of the Alamo, or, at best, seated on the ground. Fortunately there was plenty of food, simple though it was. The cattle that had been driven into the Alamo on the first day of the siege were butchered one by one and provided a constant supply of fresh meat, and there was plenty of dried corn. It was either ground and made into rough corncakes or, when there was no time for this, it was eaten dry, kernel by kernel by the men on the rifle platforms and at the artillery positions.

On the day after Robert Brown and Charles Despallier successfully set fire to the shacks on the exposed west and south sides of the Alamo, Colonel Travis sent others out to destroy those on the protected north and east sides. Usable lumber from these was hauled back inside the fortress to construct still more gun scaffolds and rifle platforms inside the walls and within the ruined towers of the mission church.

Each day the Mexican lines drew a little closer, and their fire became more effective. Heavy cannon balls thudded against the thick walls of the Alamo, breaking off fragments of stone, which buzzed through the air like angry bees. Then there would be random shots — charges made up of bits of chain and iron and smaller lead balls that sang through the air and were a greater danger to the men on the rifle platforms.

Crockett and his Tennesseeans seemed never to sleep, eat, or leave their platform on the low exposed wall. After one cannonburst Thimblerig gave a yell and tumbled backward off the platform.

Crockett jumped down and ran to his side.

"Where did it hit you?"

Thimblerig pointed to his left shoulder. Crockett tore the clothing away and probed delicately with his fingers. He held up a lead ball about the size of a hickory nut.

"Here it is," Crockett said. "If I didn't know better I'd say you'd been living right. Didn't even break the skin. Just tore up some of your fine clothes. And you might turn a little lame in that shoulder in a few days."

He turned the ball in his fingers. "You can drill a little hole in this here ball and put it on a chain and wear it for a watch fob. And you can tell your grandchildren how you stopped a ball at the Alamo."

Thimblerig smiled. "Colonel, I don't think that's practical, and I'm a practical man. I've got a better idea." He got up, took the ball, and walked toward the storeroom where rifle balls were molded and gunpowder rationed out.

Crockett climbed back to his platform, peered over the edge, and said, "Looks like something's up, boys.

Keep your eyes as sharp as lizards' and we'll see what old Santy Anny does next."

A detachment of Mexican soldiers was moving toward the Alamo at a run, driving ahead of them two teams of mules, each team hauling a small cannon. Some of the soldiers carried rifles; others carried spades and shovels. They were going to try to establish a forward artillery position.

"Wait for the order to fire," said Crockett coolly. "We'll take the mules first and the men second. That ain't the way we'd arrange a social gathering back in Tennessee, but this ain't a social gathering and it sure ain't Tennessee. Four rounds will take care of the mules." He gave orders to four of his riflemen and then turned to watch the approaching Mexicans.

They were running with their heads down. When they were within range Crockett said, "Farewell mules," and gave the order to fire. The four mules bucked and pitched in their harness and fell to the ground. One of the gun carriages overturned and the other ran on top of the body of one of the mules. "Now pick your men and let them have it," said Crockett. "There's no hurry."

The Tennesseeans squinted down the long barrels of their rifles, squeezed their triggers, and the Mexicans began to drop. The Mexican riflemen tried to take shelter behind the mules and gun carriages and trained their rifles on the Alamo, but except for an occasional head popping above the wall and down again they had no targets. The Mexicans with spades and shovels were digging furiously, trying to throw up a protecting embankment, while others tried to disentangle the gun carriages from the dead mules.

Thimblerig climbed back on the platform. "Colonel," he said to Crockett, "would you mind ordering a cease-fire?"

"Why?" Crockett demanded.

"Only until I can have five shots all to myself." He held out his hand. In it were five rifle balls. "I just molded them," said Thimblerig, "out of that stray ball that some Mexican thoughtlessly hit me with."

Crockett laughed and ordered his men to cease fire.

"But, my friend," he said to Thimblerig, "I would counsel you to take off that tall white hat of yours. Even a Mexican could hit that."

Thimblerig was loading his rifle. He solemnly took off the hat, took a position on the platform, leveled his rifle, sighted, and fired.

"One," he said, stepped back, squatted down, and reloaded.

"Two." And he continued through five.

"Five for five," said Crockett. "Right smart shooting. That's what's known as returning their fire in the very truest fashion." He ordered the rest of the Tennesseeans to resume firing.

By this time several dozen dead Mexicans lay scattered around the mules, and a Mexican officer ordered the survivors to retreat, leaving the artillery pieces.

"Maybe," said one of the Tennesseeans to Crockett, pointing at the artillery pieces, "maybe in the night we can go out and bring in those guns."

"Might as well bring in the dead mules," said Crockett. "We've not enough powder for the guns we have, so why should we bring in two more mouths to feed?"

15

The Last Reinforcements

I⊤ ᴡᴀꜱ ᴛʜᴇ ɴɪɢʜᴛ of March 1. The siege of the Alamo was eight days old. Sometime after midnight a sentry on the east, or rear, wall of the Alamo heard a slight rustle in the brush below and beyond him. Were the Mexicans planning a surprise attack? He stared into the darkness. Finally he saw a slight movement, and almost without thinking he fired his rifle, knowing that even if he didn't hit his target the report of the rifle would quickly bring others to his side.

There was a low moan in the darkness, and almost immediately there was the pounding of many feet and shouts of "Let us in, let us in! We are friends. Gonzales! Gonzales volunteers!"

The accents were unmistakably those of friends.

The men of the Alamo swung open the gate and the newcomers hurried in — one of them limping on a bleeding foot where the sentry's chance shot had caught him. The defenders of the fortress and the newcomers hugged each other with shouts of joy; but the men on the gate still held it open, peering into the darkness.

"Is that all?" they asked. It was. These were the thirty-two men who had come from Gonzales, the last reinforcements the Alamo was to receive.

They were led by Captain Albert Martin, who had been in the Alamo earlier and had gone out as a courier on the second day of the siege. Martin, a thirty-two-year-old Tennesseean, had been living in Gonzales when the fighting started. On the back of the message he had carried from Travis he had added a note of his own: "Since the above was written I have heard a heavy cannonade during the whole day. I think there must have been an attack on the Alamo. We were short of ammunition when I left. Hurry on all the men you can get in haste."

He had delivered the messages, Travis' and his own, to Andrew Ponton in Gonzales and then busied himself rounding up volunteers. He appointed a younger man, George C. Kimbell, as his lieutenant, and they sent messages to all nearby settlements pleading for volunteers to come quickly forward.

Men had begun to drift into Gonzales. There was still hope that Colonel Fannin at Goliad would send reinforcements too, but the men of Gonzales decided they could not wait for that. John W. Smith, who, with Dr. Sutherland, had first sighted Santa Anna's army approaching San Antonio and had gone out as a courier on the first day of the siege, was on hand and helped organize the volunteers. Since he was familiar with San Antonio and the country around it, he was to guide the new men into the Alamo.

The volunteers were young and old; Martin turned no one back. Some were fearful. When one of the youngsters asked Martin how they would get out of the Alamo once they were in it, Martin said good-naturedly: "Wait until we get in and then we'll figure out how to get out again."

When others, older and wiser, asked him what the chances of survival would be he told them quite honestly that they were small. But, he said, honor left them no alternative other than to go to the aid of the comrades. Their effort might be hopeless, but it would, at the very least, help slow Santa Anna's progress. Once the Alamo fell, if it fell, Santa Anna would surely move eastward and would level Gonzales to the ground. Had not Gonzales been a thorn in the

Mexicans' side from the outset? Any delay they could purchase with their lives would give their wives and children a greater opportunity to flee. And, who knew? if Fannin sent reinforcements, the tide might turn.

Finally, on Sunday, February 28 the thirty-two men of Gonzales moved toward the west and San Antonio, advancing under their own battle flag, the old piece of a white silk wedding dress with a crudely drawn picture of the town's cannon and the crudely lettered but defiant motto: "Come and Take It."

Their approach to the Alamo was slow and cautious. They were within sight of it at dusk on March 1— and also within sight of Mexican detachments guarding the eastern approach. They waited until after

midnight and then advanced, as stealthily as the Indians many of them had often fought, creeping along irrigation ditches, waiting long, suspenseful minutes to make certain they were not detected. The Alamo sentry's chance shot, however, was a signal for them to break and run for the fortress walls.

Inside the walls any foreboding the Gonzales men had about their venture seemed to disappear. Large cooking fires were built and slabs of fresh beef brought out as a meal for the newcomers. The Gonzales men held reunions with old friends. While their addition to the Alamo garrison left the total number of men less than 200, still they were pleased that of all the towns and settlements in Texas, Gonzales had the most men

in the Alamo—more than forty. They nailed their "Come and Take It" flag to a pole, ready to hoist above the Alamo walls when daylight came.

Captain Martin reported to Colonel Travis.

"You've brought only thirty-two men?" Travis asked.

"We were lucky to get that many," Martin replied. "We appealed everywhere and we took all who came. We rejected no one."

"I meant no criticism," Travis said. "It is only that the enemy outnumbers us by thirty or forty to one. What do you hear of Fannin? Is he marching to our aid?"

"We had no reports," said Martin, "that he was preparing an expedition. But we know nothing for certain. And it seemed that our wisest course was to get here with all haste and not try to join forces with Colonel Fannin."

"You had no trouble getting in?"

"Only from your own sentries. No Mexican shots were fired. It might seem that Santa Anna let us come in freely, wanting more fish in the net when he pulls the string."

"And did you bring us gunpowder?"

"Only what each man could carry in a powder horn. And this, I might say, was all the powder there was in Gonzales."

16

Encircled

On March 3, the tenth day of the siege, Bonham returned from his mission to Goliad and Gonzales. He had fixed a white handkerchief to his hat as an identifying mark, and in the middle of the day he came riding his heavily lathered cream-colored horse at a full run toward the walls of the Alamo. He had ridden full tilt past Mexican scouts, patrols, cavalrymen, and the sentries that were by now stationed quite close to the Alamo. No one attempted to stop him. It may have been, as Captain Martin had suggested earlier, that Santa Anna was anxious to get as many men in his trap as possible.

The gate swung closed behind Bonham — for the last time.

Bonham jumped from his horse, turned him loose in the court, and ran to the north wall, where his friend Travis was just putting fire to the touchhole of an eight-pound cannon. He stepped back. The cannon roared and the wall trembled. Travis waited for the smoke to clear, then peered over the wall and shook his head wearily.

"Ah, Bonham," he said. His eyes were red-rimmed, his face blackened with gunpowder, and his cheeks were hollow. There was a tremor in the right hand extended to Bonham. "Welcome back."

"The Gonzales volunteers, did they arrive?" asked Bonham.

Travis nodded and gestured toward the barracks.

There, nailed to a pole, was the Gonzales "Come and Take It" flag.

"Yes," said Travis, "they are here and very welcome. But what about Fannin and the troops from Goliad?"

"They—" Bonham started. Just then there was a tremendous blast outside the walls; the whole north wall seemed to shake. Bits of stone whizzed around them and the air was full of dust from the crumbling walls.

"Their artillery has drawn in much closer since you left," said Travis. "One gets accustomed to it. They are trying to make a breach in the walls, but thus far the walls have held. What about Fannin?"

"He — they — " Bonham began again.

"Never mind," said Travis. "If they were coming you would have told me in your first breath. Come, let me show you what has happened while you have been away."

The two men walked across the main court and the smaller court and climbed into one of the ruined church towers, from which they could see in all directions. Travis handed Bonham a battered brass spyglass.

"There to the south at about a thousand yards is their headquarters, where the flag is flying. The day before yesterday we chanced two twelve-pound shots on it. One of them struck the house, but it apparently has made no difference. We later could observe — just beyond rifle range — Santa Anna himself, walking around in his fine uniform, inspecting the damage.

"Between the headquarters and the Alamo, not more than three hundred yards from our gate, is a battery which has been very effective. Colonel Crockett and his riflemen managed to make it a costly maneuver for the enemy, but they finally got it in operation."

He pointed to the west. "We do not know how much strength there is in the town of Bexar. There is occasional artillery fire in that quarter and there are troop movements; but we are more concerned with matters close at hand."

He pointed to the north. "There is a battery which was installed this morning before dawn. It is within pistol shot of our walls. I was firing at it when you arrived. Without effect, unfortunately. A little beyond it and to the right are many entrenchments, near the old mill site. And just to the right of the entrenchments there is another artillery battery, at eight hundred yards. It has been peppering us since the day you left.

"To the east there is first the battalion of Ximenes and then the battalion of Allende, and then the cavalry posted on the Gonzales road. But I presume you know this better than I, having ridden through them.

"And there to the southeast at the old powder house is another battery, but it has been there since before you departed. And beyond it and Santa Anna's headquarters are the reinforcements—some thousands of them."

Bonham had boxed the compass with the spyglass, following Travis' explanation.

"It's hopeless, then, isn't it?" he asked.

Travis shrugged and did not answer.

But a little later Travis composed a letter to the

convention in Washington-on-the-Brazos. It was the last communication that was to come from the Alamo, and it showed just how hopeless matters were:

> To the President of the Convention,
>
> Sir: In the present confusion of the military authorities of the country, and in the absence of the commander-in-chief, I beg leave to communicate to you the situation of this garrison.
>
> From February 25 to the present date the enemy have kept up a bombardment ... I have fortified this place so that the walls are generally proof against cannon balls; and I shall continue to entrench on the inside, and strengthen the walls by throwing up dirt. At least two hundred shells have fallen inside of our works without having injured a single man; indeed, we have been so fortunate as not to lose a single man from any cause, and we have killed many of the enemy. The spirits of my men are still high, although they have had much to depress them. We have contended for ten days against an enemy whose numbers are variously estimated from fifteen hundred to six thousand men ... A reinforcement of about one thousand men is now entering Bexar from the west ...
>
> I look to the colonies alone for aid; unless it

arrives soon, I shall have to fight the enemy on his own terms . . .

If . . . reinforcements are hastened to this frontier, this neighborhood will be a great and decisive ground. The power of Santa Anna is to be met here or in the colonies; we had better meet them here than suffer a war of devastation to rage in our settlements. A blood-red banner waves from the church in Bexar . . . in token that the war is one of vengeance against rebels; they have declared us as such, demanded that we should surrender at discretion, or that this garrison should be put to the sword. Their threats have no influence on me or my men but to make all fight with desperation and that high-souled courage that characterizes the patriot who is willing to die in defense of his country's liberty and his own honor . . .

The bearer of this will give your honorable body a statement more in detail, should he escape through the enemy's lines.

God and Texas — Victory or Death.

Your Obedient Servant

W. BARRET TRAVIS, Lieut.-Col. Com.

P.S. The enemy's troops are still arriving, and the reinforcements will probably amount to two or three thousand. T.

Travis waved the letter to dry the ink, and with it still in his hand walked into the next room. A man was sitting on the floor, leaning against the rough wall, his head nodding. It was John W. Smith, the scout who had returned with the Gonzales volunteers.

"Are you awake, Smith?"

"Yes, sir." Smith staggered to his feet.

"Are you willing to undertake one last mission?"

"Of course, sir."

"I'm certain it will be the last, and getting through the lines now will be more difficult than ever before."

"No matter, sir."

"Then take this. Try to get it to the convention at Washington "

Smith took the paper, folded it, and stuffed it inside his buckskin shirt.

"'And tell them," Travis continued, "that they must make a declaration of independence. Then we will understand and the world will understand what we are fighting for.

"And tell them, Smith, that if independence is not declared I shall lay down my arms, and so will the men under my command. But if we fight under a flag of independence, we are ready to peril our lives a hundred times a day, fighting this frightful enemy who threatens to murder all prisoners and make Texas a desert waste.

"If our countrymen do not rally to our relief, then our bones will reproach our country with her neglect."

The two men left the barracks together and walked slowly toward the rear of the Alamo, where it might be possible to get across the wall and escape with safety. As they crossed the court other men approached Smith. All were haggard. Many spoke briefly, mentioned the name of a relative or friend. Others handed him bits of paper on which they had scribbled messages. Smith agreed to do what he could to deliver the messages.

David Crockett approached him and handed him a piece of paper. "This is for my children," he said, "if you would be so kind. Reporting on the balminess of the climate, their father's exuberant health, and the good hunting to be had."

Smith stuffed Crockett's message inside his shirt with the other messages, and daubed at his eyes with his buckskin sleeve.

"A little thawing around the eyes," said Crockett. "Bless you, and a happy journey."

17

The Story of Moses Rose

ACCORDING TO most serious historians, John W. Smith was the last man to leave the Alamo.

But there may have been another who was there until the last days and lived to tell about it.

The story is told that after Bonham's return and Smith's departure Travis called all his men together in the large open court of the Alamo. Until now he had concealed from his followers the fact that no more reinforcements were coming. Now he told them everything.

He explained that the constitutional convention was meeting in Washington-on-the-Brazos to form a government and create an army. But it was doubtful that anything could be done in time to aid the men in the Alamo in their perilous position. It could not be expected.

Colonel Fannin at Goliad, he had told them, had his own problems and very likely was involved in fighting Mexicans on that front. Whatever bitterness Travis may personally have felt toward Fannin and his failure to send help, he did not tell his men.

There was, he said, nothing upon which they could rely but their own spirit and bravery. Their fate was near, perhaps no more than hours away. Their only encouragement must come from the knowledge of what they were doing for Texas. For themselves there was no hope.

Travis had lined his men up in parade formation in the courtyard before he spoke, and he stood facing them. Now he walked to one end of the line, and with the sword he always carried he drew a line in the packed earth, starting at one end of the file and slowly walking to the other end, cutting a straight groove that separated the commanding officer from his men.

He could not, he said, impose a death sentence on any man in such a situation. If any man cared to attempt escape from the Alamo before the inevitable end, he was at liberty to do so. Escape would be difficult but it need not be impossible.

Those who stayed with him, he said, would defend the Alamo to the last, killing the enemy even as the enemy killed them. Surrender was impossible. Would those who were thus willing to die with him step across to his side of the line?

The entire file of men moved across the line in a body. David Crockett of Tennessee. Samuel Holloway of Philadelphia. James Kenny of Virginia. Lewis Johnson of Wales. William Harrison of Ohio. Toribio Domingo Losoyo of San Antonio. Albert Calvin Grimes of Georgia. John Hubbard Forsyth of New York. Robert Evans of Ireland. Gregorio Esparza of San Antonio. Stephen Dennison of England. George Butler of Missouri. John McGregor of Scotland. William Carey of Virginia. Henry Thomas of Germany. And all the men from Louisiana, Massachusetts, the Carolinas, Arkansas, Kentucky, Mississippi, and Ohio who had in a hundred different ways followed the trails that led to the Alamo.

Finally, only two men were left on the far side of the line.

One was the great Jim Bowie, wasted in illness, near death, but still with his bowie knife in his belt and his two pistols at his side. His comrades had carried him on his cot into the open courtyard for the meeting. Now he raised his head weakly and asked his companions to carry him across the line. This they did, ducking their heads to hide the tears in their eyes.

The other man was Moses Rose. Rose was a European, a veteran of the Napoleonic wars, who had come to the New World in the hope of leaving war and strife forever. He had settled in Nacogdoches and now, ironically, he had been thrust into still another war — and, worse, a hopeless one.

Rose was older than most of the men there, older, possibly, than all of them with the exception of David Crockett, who was fifty.

Travis and his men stared at Rose. Jim Bowie, an old friend of Rose, looked questioningly at him. Rose said simply that he was not ready to die. David Crockett, in kindly tones, told him that he might as well accept it; there was no other way.

Rose shook his head, went into the barracks, returned with a small bundle of clothing, climbed the wall, and dropped to the outside. On the ground below he stumbled and his bundle of clothing fell in a pool of Mexican blood. He picked it up and hurried away. Miraculously there was no gunfire. If the Mexicans saw him, they paid no attention.

Many days later he appeared at the home of friends in Nacogdoches. The soiled shirts in his bundle were glued together by dried blood. He told the story of

Colonel Travis and his line, and the story was handed down from generation to generation in the family.

It may have been true, or it may have been one of the legends that always grow up around great heroic events. It can never be wholly proved or disproved. Because all the other men involved in the incident were soon to die.

But if the story is not true in fact, it is true in spirit. Whether there was a line drawn on the ground in the Alamo courtyard or not, all the men there had stepped across a line, never to return.

18

The Last Day

By the twelfth day of the siege, Saturday, March 5, the men in the Alamo were near exhaustion. The Mexican lines had drawn closer on all sides, a tightening noose.

Only the fact that the Mexicans were still waiting for the heavy artillery had spared the Texans thus far. The small-caliber Mexican guns had made only one breach in the Alamo walls, on the northeast corner, and it was a small one. Travis himself guarded this corner night and day, loading and firing the eight-pound cannon himself.

There was no rest for the 187 men. To man the walls properly and in usual military fashion would have taken at least five times their number. There was no relief. Men stayed at their posts night and day, grimy, red-eyed, increasingly short of temper as their nerves became more strained. When there was a lull in the fighting they could catnap without leaving their positions, often without sitting down.

Saturday, March 5, was a bitterly cold day. A north wind chilled the men to the bone; puddles of water had a thin skin of ice. The Texans cursed the weather with as much vehemence as they cursed the Mexicans.

But suddenly, without explanation, the Mexican cannonading ceased. So did the musket fire that came sporadically from the encircling lines.

The Texans waited with as much alertness as they could muster for the firing to resume. Meanwhile they held their own fire. There was too little powder left to fire when no one was firing at them.

Fifteen minutes went by. A half-hour. An hour. Gradually the Texans relaxed. Many slumped against the wall; others slid into sitting positions on the firing platform. And all of them dozed. Darkness came and still they slept, exhausted from almost two weeks of tension without sleep. The usual picket sentries were placed outside the walls of the Alamo to warn if there was an attack, but even they moved like sleepwalkers in the cold.

What had happened?

Santa Anna well knew the condition of the Texans. He knew that with any excuse they would give in to the exhaustion they had thus far fought off just as they had fought off the Mexicans. In this way they could be surprised — and Santa Anna planned to surprise them. He was impatient for victory. This was taking too much time. Six thousand troops should have vanquished less than 200 men in twelve minutes. It had now been twelve days.

Members of his staff wanted to wait until heavier artillery could be received from Mexico. Then the walls of the Alamo could be hammered down and its defenders exposed.

Santa Anna overruled them. The Alamo would be taken by storm on all sides. He issued orders. All men were to retire at sundown, arise at midnight, and go to their stations. More than 2000 men would be used as shock troops. Divided into four columns they would, at the signal, race toward the Alamo from four different directions, each column equipped with scaling ladders. The cavalry was to be stationed farther back, to cut off any attempt at flight, either on the part of the Texans or the Mexicans themselves — for Santa Anna had suffered many desertions early in the expedition. Behind the cavalry would be the artillery and thousands of reserves.

Santa Anna knew his casualties would be heavy, and he cautioned his officers of this. There would be great bloodshed, but this was not to deter them; whatever was required in terms of lives, the Alamo must be taken — for the honor of the Mexican government and of Santa Anna himself. And, he cautioned his officers, there would be no prisoners. Some, knowing the usual rules of warfare, asked him to repeat this. "No prisoners," said Santa Anna. "They are all traitors and must be put to traitor's death."

The night was cold and still. Within the Alamo the Texans slept as though drugged. The picket sentries outside the Alamo were easily overcome by stealthy-footed Mexicans. At his headquarters, five hundred yards away, Santa Anna, who had been up all night drinking coffee and checking all details of his plan of attack, gave the signal.

A Mexican bugler blew an eerie call on his bugle. It was the *degüello,* a call to battle the Spaniards had learned centuries before from their old enemies the Moors. It meant "attack with no quarter," just as had the red flag Santa Anna had run up on San Fernando tower thirteen days before warned the men in the Alamo that no mercy was to be shown to them.

Thousands of feet began drumming across the

frozen ground, and the men in the Alamo stirred and woke.

A Mexican volunteer in the Alamo awakened and ran to the side of Colonel Travis, asleep by his cannon on the north wall. He shook him by the shoulder and stammered, "*Es el degüello, mi coronel.*"

Travis leaped to his feet, bewildered. "What is the *degüello?*" But he knew almost before the man told him and was readying a match at the touch hole of his cannon. The cannon ball, he could see in the dim light, cut a wide swath through the Mexicans that were now pouring toward the Alamo. Still they came.

Bonham was manning three artillery pieces from platforms built in the old mission church in the Alamo. The cannon were so mounted that they could shoot in three different directions, and their fire was effective and deadly at first. Neither Bonham's cannon nor other artillery in the Alamo could shoot downward, and now the attacking Mexicans were under the very walls, preparing to scale them.

The riflemen had all jumped to their stations and were firing, reloading and firing at a rapid clip. But with the Mexicans directly below them at the base of the walls, they could not protect themselves. If they stood on the platforms within the walls they could not aim at the men nearest them. They had to get on top of the walls in order to fire on the Mexicans below them, and in so doing they exposed themselves to enemy fire. One Texan after another began to drop, the first casualties since the beginning of the siege. This did not deter them. David Crockett and his Tennesseeans were particularly effective. The largest pile of dead and wounded Mexicans accumulated under the stockade fence to which Crockett and his men had been assigned. Crockett himself was cool and daring. He would fire and, without taking shelter, casually reload in full view of the Mexicans.

The Mexicans paid no heed to their own dead and wounded. Urged on by their officers, they advanced over the bodies of their comrades, crushing the dead and the wounded alike. Finally they had their scaling ladders in place against the walls and began to clamber up and over.

They were coming too fast now for the Texans to pick them off with rifle fire. The Texans used their rifles as clubs, knocking the Mexicans from the walls. When the rifles broke they would cut and stab with their bowie knives. Yet the Mexicans came on, and now they were dropping into the courtyard of the Alamo.

The artillerymen on the walls swung their guns so that they were pointed within the Alamo itself, and fired away, for there were now far more Mexicans within the Alamo than there were Texans.

Travis fell beside his cannon, a musket ball in his head. As a Mexican officer approached him he made a final convulsive effort and thrust his sword into the enemy; the two men died together.

David Crockett had one arm shattered by a musket ball. He continued firing with only one arm at point-blank range, and then, as he was surrounded on the wall, used Old Betsy as a club, swinging wildly about him and knocking Mexicans about like tenpins. The rifle broke. He dropped it and went at the enemy with his knife, until a sword thrust dropped him.

In the Alamo courtyard the Texans, greatly reduced in numbers, retreated to the long barracks, which they had previously strengthened with sandbags. They closed and secured the doors as soon as they were inside. But the Mexicans, now in possession of the Texas artillery pieces, swung them around, charged them, and shot away the doors of the barracks. The Mexicans then pursued the Texans, going from room to room, killing as they went. A frenzy had taken hold of them now. All had bayonets on their rifles, and in their madness they would toss the bodies of their victims from one to another on the bayonets.

Bonham had fallen across one of the cannon he

was firing. Jim Bowie had been taken on his cot to the baptistry of the old mission church, where he was being cared for by the half-dozen women who had taken shelter in the Alamo. The fighting had awakened him and when the Mexicans began to enter the room he was ready, his pistols cocked and pointed. He shot the first Mexican who attempted to enter. The others hesitated, and Bowie reloaded. A second came in. Bowie killed him and reloaded. A pile of Mexican bodies accumulated by the door. Finally the Mexicans rushed the room. Bowie killed two more, but there was no time to reload. Drawing the bowie knife that he had worn at his belt all through his illness, he wielded it dangerously until a Mexican bayonet was plunged into him.

Dawn came, and within a short time the thirteen-day defense of the Alamo was at an end. Santa Anna had waited at his headquarters during the assault. When daylight came and the fighting seemed to have ceased, he ventured out and walked toward the fortress. Everywhere the ground was covered with the bodies of his troops, many of them crushed beyond recognition. Santa Anna marched along with his head up, ignoring the dismal scene. But as he approached the walls a rifle shot rang out of the Alamo, and a ball whistled over his head. He retired to his headquarters.

All of the Texans were dead, but shooting still continued in the Alamo. Some of the Mexicans, hysterical from the carnage and confused in the smoke-filled dark rooms, were continuing to fire at each other.

Finally it was at an end. Santa Anna walked through the Alamo and asked to be shown the bodies of Travis, Crockett, Bonham, and Bowie. He gave orders that the bodies of Mexican dead were to be carefully separated from the Texans. The bodies of the Texans were then piled in a great funeral pyre and burned, while the townspeople of San Antonio attended to the burial of the Mexicans.

It had been a costly victory. The 187 Texans who defended the Alamo with their lives had killed approximately 1600 of Santa Anna's men — almost ten for one.

In his report of the battle, sent back to Mexico by courier, Santa Anna said the Alamo had been defended by "more than six hundred foreigners." They had, he said, been conquered at a cost of 70 Mexican dead and 300 wounded. Whatever else the defenders of the Alamo had accomplished, they had at least compelled the self-styled Napoleon of the West to juggle the figures in order to look better in the eyes of his countrymen.

19

Independence

WASHINGTON-ON-THE-BRAZOS was a raw new settlement situated on a red clay bluff overhanging the Brazos River. The cold rains of February had swollen the river until it was an ugly yellow torrent. A ferry plied back and forth in constant danger of capsizing. There were a dozen or so log cabins in the village, two of them, only slightly larger than the rest, identified by signs as "hotels."

In the last days of February men from all the Texas colonies began gathering in Washington, as they called it. There were men with frock coats and fine hats and men in homespun and buckskin. No matter what their clothing, it was soaked with rain and caked with mud. The lucky ones found places for sleep in the so-called hotels. Others were given floor space in the private cabins. Others bedded themselves down in a provisions store, in a saloon, in a carpenter's shop.

They were delegates to the Texas constitutional convention. Some had been of the "war party," which wanted an outright break with Mexico, and others had belonged to the "peace party," which wanted only reforms. There had been bitter personal differences, but now they were forgotten. Santa Anna had changed everything.

Sam Houston was among the last of the delegates to arrive. He rode into Washington from the east on Monday, February 29 (it was leap year), and the convention was to meet the following day. Houston was

riding a Spanish pony. His feet almost touched the ground. He wore buckskin clothing and Indian moccasins and had a brightly colored Indian blanket wrapped tightly about him.

He was immediately surrounded by delegates, who nervously asked if he had heard the news of Santa Anna and the siege of the Alamo. They had already received Travis' first message from the Alamo. The delegates, to a man, were in favor of arming themselves and riding to the relief of their comrades.

Houston held up his hand. They must, he said, attend to the business for which they were assembled. Until Texas had a government things would continue in the same chaotic pattern. There must be a declaration of independence and an election of governing officers.

Some of the delegates complained, but they followed Houston's advice. The next day, March 1, they assembled in an unfinished meeting hall, seating themselves on benches hewn from logs. Cotton cloth was nailed over the open windows to shield them from the wind and the rain. Tallow candles did little to lessen the gloom, and there was no heat.

Travis' message of February 24, addressed "To the People of Texas & all Americans in the world" was read to the convention. Most of the delegates knew

about it already, but again there was a strong surge
of feeling and many demands that the convention
recess so that its members could ride to the relief of
the Alamo. And again the counsel of Houston pre-
vailed. By the next a declaration of independence had
been drawn up.

> The Mexican government [it read], by its col-
> onization laws, invited and induced the Anglo-
> American population of Texas to colonize its
> wilderness, under pledged faith of a written
> Constitution, that they should continue to enjoy
> that constitutional liberty and republican gov-
> ernment to which they had been habituated in
> the land of their birth, the United States of
> America. In this expectation they have been
> cruelly disappointed, inasmuch as the Mexican
> nation has acquiesced in the late changes made
> in the government by Gen. Antonio Lopez de
> Santa Anna, who, having overturned the Con-
> stitution of his country, now offers us the cruel
> alternative, either to abandon our homes, ac-
> quired by so many privations, or submit to the
> most intolerable of all tyranny.
>
> It has sacrificed our welfare . . .
>
> It has failed and refused to secure, on a firm
> basis, the right of trial by jury . . .

It has failed to establish any public system of education . . .

It has suffered the military commandants stationed among us to exercise arbitrary acts of oppression and tyranny . . .

It has demanded us to deliver up our arms, which are essential to our defense . . .

It has invaded our country, both by sea and by land, with intent to lay waste our territory, and drive us from our homes; and has now a large mercenary army advancing to carry on against us a war of extermination . . .

The fifty-nine signers included names such as Ruiz, Navarro, and Zavala, along with the plain Anglo-American names. Sam Houston signed in a script as large and flourishing as that with which John Hancock signed the American Declaration of Independence.

The "large mercenary army" was by this time applying unbearable pressure to the defenders of the Alamo. On the same day that the declaration was signed, Travis sent out his last message from the Alamo, ending it "God and Texas — Victory or Death." When it reached the convention there once more were demands that the delegates march on the Alamo. Houston again calmed them, urged them to continue their work. He had by then been officially named commander-in-chief of the nonexistent Texas army.

Houston took his leave of the convention, assuring the delegates that he would go to the Alamo and do all in his power to help the men there. He rode out of Washington with his aide, George Hockley, and three volunteers. Houston realized there was little he and his four companions could do unless more volunteers could be found; but the gesture satisfied the convention. The convention proceeded with the details of establishing a provisional government.

The five men rode west as fast as their horses could carry them in the mud. At times Houston, in Indian fashion, would dismount and place his ear to the

ground. Finally he said, "The guns of the Alamo are silenced."

"Then we are too late," said one of the men.

"No," said Houston. "This is only the beginning. May I remind you of a line written by Colonel Travis in one of his dispatches? 'The victory,' he wrote, 'will cost the enemy so dear that it will be worse for him than defeat.' Our duty now is to prove it."

20

Flight to the East

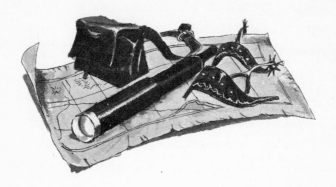

WHEN HOUSTON and his few companions arrived in Gonzales they found there 175 volunteers who had come from other parts of the colonies, ready to go to the Alamo. They had two cannon, and other volunteers were drifting in.

The commander-in-chief had just started to form the men into squads and instruct them in drill and maneuvers when there was a great outcry in the town of Gonzales.

Two Mexicans had ridden into town with the news that the Alamo had fallen, that Santa Anna had killed all its defenders. The women of the town were wailing; most of them were now widows. Houston declared the two Mexicans were spies, sent by Santa

Anna to spread panic, and ordered them arrested. Secretly he was certain that the tale they told was true. While he tried to calm both townspeople and volunteers, he dispatched orders to Fannin at Goliad to blow up Fort Defiance, sink his artillery pieces in the river, destroy any surplus powder, and retreat. He also sent word to the constitutional convention.

He continued drilling his volunteers. They had now increased to more than 500. A day or so later a famed Indian fighter and scout named Deaf Smith rode into camp, bringing with him Mrs. Almaron Dickerson, her baby daughter, Angelina, and a young Negro named Joe. All three were survivors of the Alamo.

Mrs. Dickerson's husband had been killed fighting there. Joe had been the servant of Colonel Travis. All had been spared by Santa Anna and sent on their way to carry news to the rest of Texas of what had happened at the Alamo. Mrs. Dickerson had been asked to convey Santa Anna's compliments to Houston and assure him that all Texans who resisted the Mexican authority would meet the same fate.

Santa Anna's gesture had the desired effect. The townspeople and many of the volunteers became hysterical. Twenty of the volunteers deserted and fled eastward through Texas, spreading the news as they went. Panic spread like a prairie fire, and soon most

of the colonists were fleeing eastward. Santa Anna, they were certain, would soon be on their trail. Even the delegates to the convention at Washington-on-the-Brazos wanted to run for their lives. Only David G. Burnet succeeded in calming them, and as a result was elected provisional president of the new Republic of Texas.

Houston organized his own force for retreat. Artillery pieces were sunk in the Guadalupe River. Most of the wagons were destroyed. The volunteer force, now increased to almost 800, moved east under the cover of night with refugees moving along with them.

Houston was everywhere at once. He reassured the refugees and volunteers alike. He beat a drum for the men to rise in the morning. He once repaired a faulty musket for a young volunteer. And if he had a plan of strategy he told no one.

Hotheads among his followers were restless, insisted that Houston should reverse his path and attack the enemy. One column of Santa Anna's forces pursued them. No sooner had Houston and his followers crossed the Colorado River than the Mexicans appeared on the shore they had just left. Many of the younger Texans insisted that they be permitted to attack. Houston refused. A victory there, he said, would not be decisive. And a loss could be disastrous.

That night, leaving their campfires burning so the Mexicans would not suspect, they moved on to the east again.

Some of the younger officers talked of mutiny; of calling a meeting of all volunteers and ousting Houston as their commander, putting in his place someone more aggressive, more inclined to take the fight to the enemy.

Houston went about his own business.

Spring had come. The struggling column moved slowly through groves of oak and mesquite and across prairies of new green grass. More volunteers joined the column, and two matching six-pound cannon, a gift of the citizens of Cincinnati, were received and christened "The Twin Sisters." The column stopped at plantations where there were ample food supplies to rest, repair equipment, and go through more drills. Gradually the ragged band of volunteers was beginning to look and behave like the army that Texas so badly needed.

Disheartening news came during the march. The only other Texas military force was that commanded by Colonel Fannin at Goliad. Now it was lost. Just as he had paid little heed to the pleas to come to the relief of the Alamo, Fannin had ignored Houston's order to retreat from Goliad. General Urrea, advancing north from Matamoros, had wiped out two advance parties of Texans. Fannin set out with the main force of his little army to aid Texans stranded in the nearby town of Refugio, more directly in the path of Urrea's advance. They were surprised by Urrea, whose army outnumbered them three to one. After a day of fighting on Coleto Creek they surrendered to Urrea, hoping that he might be a more humane captor than was Santa Anna and would spare their lives. This Urrea might have done, but he was under Santa Anna's orders. The Texans were marched back to the fortress at Goliad, held prisoner until Palm Sunday, March 27, just three weeks after the fall of the Alamo. Then they were marched out of the fortress, thinking they were to be marched to Mexico and prison. Instead, the 342 men were shot down in cold blood, Fannin with them.

News of this outrage infuriated the men marching with Houston and there were fresh demands that they halt the retreat and go on the offensive. Again Houston ignored the demands.

Santa Anna, it was known, had moved southeast to Harrisburg, near the Gulf of Mexico, where he destroyed the temporary capitol of the new republic.

There came a day when the trail Houston's army was following branched. The branch to the right led to the south, to Harrisburg and Santa Anna's army.

The one to the left led to the Sabine River and beyond it the United States. There were rumors that Houston planned to retreat all the way to the United States in the hope that the United States would then intervene.

Just before the fork in the road was reached Houston called a halt. Then, after whispered conversations with a few of the officers he trusted, he ordered the column to advance — to the right, toward the ruins of Harrisburg, toward Santa Anna. There were cheers in the marching column as the men picked up their muskets and packs and moved off at a brisker pace.

21

The Retreat Ends

SANTA ANNA was overconfident. After the victory at the Alamo he was convinced that the Texas rebellion was really over. Only a little mopping up remained to be done, and he planned an early return to Mexico City.

He divided his army into four columns and took command of one himself. In leisurely fashion he moved eastward across Texas. The new government, he knew, had established itself in Harrisburg, a new village near the Gulf of Mexico, just below the present city of Houston.

When he reached Harrisburg the Texas government fled toward Galveston Island, just off the coast. Santa Anna and the 800 men he had with him burned

Harrisburg and pursued the fugitive government, headed by President Burnet, to the coast. Santa Anna and his men had to move slowly in the swampy coastal country, cut by many bayous and streams. They had received reports that Houston and his retreating army were headed for the Sabine River and the United States — just as many of Houston's men had thought.

The refugees who had marched along with Houston's column did head for the Sabine River and the United States frontier — and so did some of Houston's volunteer soldiers. But the main body, led by Houston, was now moving south toward the ruins of Harrisburg.

They trudged through the swampy coastal prairies, frequently bogging down in the mud. Wagons had literally to be carried on the backs of men across the many water holes. So did the two small cannon that had come from Cincinnati — too small to be of great value in a battle but too heavy to be carried in comfort.

Deaf Smith, the scout, captured two Mexican couriers and obtained the information that Santa Anna and his army were less than ten miles away, moving slowly and uncertainly in the swamp country, as was Houston's army. At one stop Houston made a speech to his men, told them that Santa Anna was near, that

they might soon be in battle. Victory, he assured them, was certain. And he concluded, "Trust in God and fear not! And remember the Alamo! Remember the Alamo!"

His men picked up the phrase and roared back at him: "Remember the Alamo! Remember the Alamo!"

Leaving the heavy baggage behind, Houston moved forward with a picked force, the ablest, most aggressive of his men. They came to a body of water identified on their maps as Buffalo Bayou. The men made a raft of the floor and roof timbers of an abandoned log cabin and the entire army poled its way across the stream and camped in a thicket. A little farther along there was another, smaller bayou, and across it was a little bridge, Vince's Bridge. Houston's army tramped across and found traces of campfires. Santa Anna and his men had been there before them. Santa Anna, who had pursued them across Texas, was now being pursued.

The Texans moved cautiously ahead in the darkness. Wagon and cannon wheels had been wrapped in rags to muffle their sound and squeaky axles were greased with beef tallow. Vigilant and silent, they dipped down into a ravine, slowly climbed out the other side, and carefully worked their way across the prairie. Now they could taste and smell the salt air from the Gulf of Mexico. At last they came to a woods and Houston gave the order to halt. The men were tired and famished. Houston gave them permission to kill some cows they found grazing and to build some fires for roasting the meat. But before this could be done scouts dashed into camp. They had, they reported, clashed with a Mexican patrol, and had learned that Santa Anna's army was on its way to Lynch's Ferry. It appeared that Santa Anna intended to cross the San Jacinto and head for the Sabine River, whither he thought Houston and his army were bound.

Houston ordered camp broken, and the tired men once more crept across the prairie, finally setting up camp in a live-oak grove near the point at which Buffalo Bayou flowed into the San Jacinto River. The Texans learned that Santa Anna was five miles to the south of them. Across the San Jacinto River to the east was the settlement of Lynchburg. Beyond it, on a hill, the Texans could see people clustered—but at the sight of the Texans they faded away. They were Mexican sympathizers, waiting for Santa Anna to cross the river, after which they would guide the Mexican army on its way to pursue the supposedly fleeing Texans.

Again cows were killed and fires built; this time the men had a feast. Two scouts had captured the ferry that plied across the San Jacinto River, and with it a supply of flour destined for Santa Anna's men. The Texans made the flour into dough strips and wound them around green willow sticks to toast in the fire. Stomachs were full, for a change, and spirits were fine. Houston's men were eager for a fight. They cleaned their guns and whetted their bowie knives on flat stones until the points were like needles, the edges like razors.

Scouts galloped into camp and said that Santa Anna and his men were just beyond a low rise to the south of the Texans, and almost as they said it a Mexican bugle call floated in the air.

The Texans ran to positions in a firing line and the twin cannon were wheeled into place. A line of Mexican skirmishers came into view on the crest of the rise, and then the full Mexican force, first the foot soldiers and then the cavalry. The lines parted and a Mexican artillery piece was wheeled through and placed in firing position.

The first of the Twin Sisters fired. It was a lucky shot. The horses that had drawn the Mexican gun both fell to the ground, their legs kicking. The officer commanding the gun was down, and the gun carriage seemed to be disabled. The second of the Twin Sisters was fired, but now the Mexicans had put their cannon back in firing order and it replied. The Mexican skirmishers fired and the Texans held their fire, waiting for them to draw closer. Instead, the Mexicans withdrew behind the rise and, suddenly, everything was quiet again.

The next morning the Texans heard reveille as usual at four o'clock, and in minutes they were in position and ready. Surely this was the day. Those who had kept track of the time knew it was April 21, 1836, and it might well be a date they would remember all their lives.

But where was General Houston? Until today he had always been up before the men, had beaten reveille on the drum himself to call them to duty. But this morning, they discovered, the general was still sleeping, his head cushioned on a coil of rope.

When he finally awakened it was bright daylight, and he wandered about the camp in casual, good-natured fashion as if there were nothing more to do than enjoy the balmy spring weather.

His followers once more began to grumble. Why had they lost the opportunity to attack? Houston paid no attention to them.

Two of the most trusted scouts, Deaf Smith and Henry Karnes, rode into the camp.

Santa Anna, Smith said in the strange, high-pitched

voice of a deaf man, was getting reinforcements, and he pointed in the direction from which he had just come. A line of pack mules could be seen moving across the grassland.

By now Houston had come up. He listened and watched and then, smiling, said to Smith, "My friend, you have fallen for one of the oldest tricks of military art. Santa Anna is marching a line of mules around and around to make it appear that he is receiving reinforcements."

The Texans laughed. If this was the case, why could they not attack at once, before Santa Anna received real reinforcements? Houston ignored them and led Deaf Smith to one side.

Out of earshot of his men Houston questioned Smith closely. They were indeed reinforcements — more than 500 men under General Cos, which would increase Santa Anna's effective force to more than 1300 as compared with the 910 men that Houston had.

Houston called for two well-sharpened axes and handed them to his scouts. Still whispering, he instructed them to return to the bridge over Vince's Bayou, across which the reinforcements had come, and destroy it. Somewhere beyond the bridge was still another and larger Mexican column — perhaps as many as 3000 men. There was no point in allowing them to get through, too. And, he added, this would also cut off any retreat for the Texans.

22

Battle of San Jacinto

Finally in midafternoon Houston, without warning, ordered his men to prepare for attack. The men eagerly took their positions, and at four o'clock Houston, mounted on a white horse, raised his sword as a signal to advance. The column of marching men moved out across the prairie, moving steadily up the gentle rise beyond which lay Santa Anna and his army. Behind them a fife played an old love song, "Will You Come to the Bower," for the army of the new Republic of Texas had no national anthem, no martial airs.

Houston rode back and forth in front of them on a white horse, cautioning them to hold their fire. Finally the advancing column crested the rise. Beyond them was a barricade the Mexicans had erected of saddles, trunks, baggage wagons, and other equipment. Behind it lay Santa Anna's camp, quiet and peaceful. Then there was the sound of a Mexican bugle and the apparently sleeping camp began to come awake. There was a burst of musket fire from behind the barricade. Houston's white horse was hit. He jumped from the saddle and swung himself onto a smaller horse, offered by one of his cavalrymen. All the time he shouted orders for his men to hold their fire.

There was a shout from the Texans' rear lines and Deaf Smith rode among them. Smith shouted, "You must fight for your lives, lads. We've cut down Vince's Bridge!"

Houston raised his hat, waved it in the air, and barked out a command, but his voice was drowned in the roar of the Texans as they surged toward the barricade, pausing only to fire at Mexicans as they appeared. Without bothering to reload, they plunged over the barricade and into the Mexican camp, swinging their rifles as clubs and flashing their bowie knives.

The Mexicans had been caught unprepared. When the Texans failed to attack at dawn they had reasoned they would not attack at all; and they were confident both in their past record against the Texans and in their reinforcements. After the midday meal most of

them had retired for a nap, leaving only a few sentries.

Santa Anna himself dashed out of his tent, where he had been resting. Wearing red slippers, he flung himself on a black horse and dashed away in the opposite direction.

The Texans now were shouting "Remember the Alamo! Remember Goliad! Remember the Alamo!" And like so many savages they flung themselves on the Mexicans. Mexican artillerymen clustered around their fieldpieces, trying to bring them into play and were clubbed to earth by the Texans. A group of Mexican cavalry tried to flee toward Vince's Bayou, where the bridge had been cut. Pursuing Texans drove them over the bank of the bayou and into the water, where most of them drowned.

The main assault was over in eighteen minutes. One column of 400 Mexicans, who had retreated in orderly fashion under the command of an able officer, marched back a few minutes later behind a white flag, ready to surrender.

Houston had his second horse shot out from under him and mounted a third. A rifle ball struck his right leg, shattering it above the ankle. Weak from loss of blood he continued riding up and down, shouting orders which his volunteers, now mad with victory, seldom heard.

The pursuit continued all over the plain of San Jacinto. Finally, as dusk fell, the Texans felt that Santa Anna's army had been destroyed.

Only 9 of the 910 Texans at San Jacinto were killed or fatally wounded and 30 or so less seriously wounded. The plain was littered with the bodies of dead Mexicans, and there were 730 Mexican prisoners.

But the most important Mexican was missing. Where was Santa Anna?

All through the next day Texans scoured the area, bringing in stray prisoners. Toward evening one party, scouting near the ruined bridge across Vince's Bayou, found a man trying to hide beneath a blanket in the tall grass. He wore a woman's blue smock and had on red slippers. To those who could understand Spanish he explained that he was just a private soldier. They brought him into camp. As they approached the prisoners' pen the other Mexicans began to shout *"El Presidente!"* And they all drew to attention facing the man in the smock. It was Santa Anna.

Angry Texans gathered around the man, their bowie knives bared, their faces scowling.

"Give him what he gave our boys at the Alamo," they shouted, and moved in a tightening circle around the man. A captain of the guard moved in, ordered the men back, and, at gun point, marched Santa Anna

to a live-oak tree, beneath which Sam Houston lay.

Houston had lost much blood from his wound and was in great pain, but he roused himself and greeted Santa Anna with courtesy. Behind him the angry Texans grumbled and debated how death should be dealt out to the villain.

With amazing poise, Santa Anna extended his compliments to General Houston. It was a great man indeed, he said, who could overcome the Napoleon of the West.

Houston brushed aside the combination of flattery and arrogance.

Why, he asked, had Santa Anna slaughtered the Texans at the Alamo?

Because, Santa Anna replied, they brought it upon themselves with their stubborn resistance, killing many Mexican troops. He had no alternative but to kill them to the last man, since they would not surrender.

Why then, asked Houston, were Fannin and his men at Goliad killed, although they had surrendered and were peaceful prisoners?

The question upset Santa Anna. He said he had no knowledge of the reasons for the action; he presumed the Mexican troops were obeying orders. But they were not his orders.

Finally Houston gave permission for Santa Anna's

tent to be erected nearby and the Mexican general was excused. Houston still lay under the tree, nibbling at grains of corn. His men pressed around him.

Why shouldn't Santa Anna be shot down like a dog, they demanded, or, better yet, hanged?

Houston chewed on the corn and was silent. Then raising his head, he explained: Santa Anna was worth more to them alive than dead. Santa Anna was not only the commander of Mexican armies in the field. He was also President of Mexico. Mexico still had an army of perhaps 3000 men in Texas, far more men than the Texans could muster. This was a grave danger to the Texans. But with Santa Anna as a hostage of the Texans, the Mexicans dared not attack, thus risking the life of their general and their president. With Santa Anna in their hands, the Texans could demand the withdrawal of the Mexicans from Texas, could negotiate a peace.

23

What the Men of the Alamo Won

SANTA ANNA, while a captive, negotiated an armistice with the Texans and ordered all Mexican soldiers to leave the new republic and withdraw beyond the Rio Grande. In time he was permitted to return to Mexico. He told his government that it was not bound by the pledges he had made, that he had made them only as an individual, not as the representative of the Mexican government. But Mexico was so involved in other problems that she made no immediate effort to reclaim the lost territory.

In years to come Santa Anna would again take to the battlefield against Americans. Matters might have been much simpler — for Mexico as well as Texas — if Sam Houston had simply turned Santa Anna over to be hung or shot by his men at San Jacinto.

Santa Anna was not Houston's only problem. David Burnet, the provisional president of Texas, both disliked Houston as a person and was jealous of his victory at San Jacinto. He refused permission for Houston to board a Texas naval vessel bound for New Orleans, where Houston had to go for surgery on the leg shattered at San Jacinto. And he dismissed from the service the Texas army surgeon who had treated Houston.

Houston made his way to New Orleans by trading schooner, was treated for his wound, and returned to Texas. The new republic was in a turmoil. Burnet was weak and confused. He trusted no one and changed his cabinet officers almost daily. He could not find the constitution that had been drawn up at Washington-on-the-Brazos and had to be submitted to citizens of Texas for approval. The army was getting out of hand. It had grown to tremendous size. Volunteers from the United States flooded in after the victory at San Jacinto — now that Texas no longer needed them. And the soldiers were clamoring for an expedition into Mexico.

Houston was the only man who commanded the respect of everyone — except Burnet — and in the first election he was overwhelmingly elected President.

He guided Texas toward annexation by the United States, twice served it as its President and later as both a United States Senator and Governor.

Texas, as part of the United States, went to war with Mexico again in 1846 over settlement of the Texas boundaries. As long as Texas was a struggling republic the Texas boundary was unimportant. But now the Texas boundary was the frontier of the United States. The United States first tried to buy Texas and the lands to the west of it, and, failing this, went to war.

The Treaty of Guadalupe Hidalgo, which ended it, gave the United States not only a clear title to Texas but to almost all of what is now California, Arizona, New Mexico, Nevada, and Utah.

All this stemmed from the 187 men who died in a hopeless fight at the Alamo. It was their desperate bravery that forced the Texans to go ahead and form a government and put an army in the field. And they gave the Texans their battle cry at San Jacinto.

It is doubtful that any of the men at the Alamo could have foreseen this. Concerned as they were with the lack of gunpowder and reinforcements and sleep, they had no time to dream of the nation they were helping to make. They were brave men in a fight, nothing more and nothing less. If they stopped to think why they were fighting, it is likely they thought of nothing more complicated than David Crockett's motto, which he often repeated to them during the thirteen days that led to death: "Be sure you're right and go ahead."

Bibliography

FOR THE YOUNG READER who wishes to know more about the beginning of Texas, the siege and defense of the Alamo, the battle of San Jacinto and the people involved, here are some books that will be helpful:

13 DAYS TO GLORY, by Lon Tinkle (New York, McGraw-Hill, 1958). One of the most complete and readable accounts of the battle of the Alamo.

THE DAY OF SAN JACINTO, by Frank X. Tolbert (New York, McGraw-Hill, 1959). Recently published, this book is a complete and exciting story of the way in which the little Texas army avenged the fall of the Alamo and the massacre of Goliad at San Jacinto.

THE RAVEN, by Marquis James (Indianapolis, Bobbs-Merrill, 1929). Though basically a biography of Sam Houston, the book gives a complete story of the early days of Texas, which Houston served as general, president, governor, and senator.

SAM HOUSTON, THE TALLEST TEXAN, by William Johnson (New York, Random House, 1953). Written by the author of this book; it is centered on the personality and leadership of Sam Houston, who was more responsible than any other individual for Texas' existence, first as an independent republic and then as a state.

STORIES OF CHRISTMAS AND THE BOWIE KNIFE, by J. Frank Dobie (Austin, Texas, Steck Co., 1953). A slim little volume, printed for private distribution, this contains a thoughtful story about the bowie knife, which was to the Alamo what Excalibur was to the world of King Arthur.

CORONADO'S CHILDREN, by J. Frank Dobie (Dallas, Texas, Southwest Press, 1930). Although not specifically concerned with the Alamo and the Texas war of independence, this book has fascinating tales about the treasure seekers, Jim Bowie among them, who came into Texas in the early days.

A SOCIAL AND POLITICAL HISTORY OF TEXAS, by Lewis W. Newton and Herbert P. Gambrell (Dallas, Texas, Southwest Press, 1932). A standard history of the state.

A HISTORY OF MEXICO, by Henry Bamford Parkes (Boston, Houghton Mifflin, 1938). The best available history of Mexico, containing much of the past history of the area that became Texas, the causes of the struggle between the Texas colonists and Mexico, and greater detail concerning Santa Anna.

THE TEXAS ALMANAC (Dallas, Texas, Dallas Morning News, published in new editions every other year). This contains a vast amount of information about Texas, both historical and current.

THE HANDBOOK OF TEXAS, Walter Prescott Webb, editor-in-chief (Austin, Texas, Texas State Historical Association, 1952, 2 vols.). Very useful for the serious student who desires more detailed information concerning persons, places, and events involved in the history of Texas.

A VISIT TO TEXAS, BEING THE JOURNEY OF A TRAVELLER THROUGH THOSE PARTS MOST INTERESTING TO AMERICAN SETTLERS (New York, Goodrich & Wiley, 1834). The journal of an anonymous Englishman who describes in great detail the appearance and character of the country shortly before the war for independence. The Steck Company of Austin, Texas, published a facsimile edition in 1952.

Davy Crockett's Own Story As Written by Himself (New York, Citadel Press, 1955). While the accuracy of this account may be in doubt, it is a picturesque story about one of the most colorful of the heroes of the Alamo.

Index

SAINT MATTHEW SCHOOL
1015 E. Dayton St.
South Bend, Ind.